LIVING PRAYER

by

Archbishop Anthony Bloom

TEMPLEGATE, PUBLISHERS
Springfield, Illinois 62705

Published in England by Darton, Longman & Todd, Ltd.
64 Chiswick High Road, London W 4

Published in the United States by Templegate, Publishers,
Springfield, Illinois 62705

CONTENTS

PREFATORY NOTE

"Lord teach us to pray." The disciples of Our Lord, even though they enjoyed the daily presence of the Savior, sought guidance in approaching the Father in prayer. Through all the centuries the same desire that motivated the disciples prompts continued search for fresh and effective ways of prayer leading to closer communion with God, our Father.

In response, and also from the days of the infant Church, there have been discussions and treatises on prayer, some pastoral, others theoretical, some of passing moment, others of classic worth, all contributing to the Christian's growth in the spiritual life. The present work is among the latest of these. It probably will not rank among the enduring classics of spiritual guidance; it makes no pretense of seeking to do so. But it does answer a perennial need in a spirit attractive to present day forms of that need.

Archbishop Bloom addresses himself to the pastoral instruction of the faithful in a meaningful approach to prayer. Old and familiar truths are presented freshly and vividly so as to make clear again simple facts sometimes found clouded.

In an age dominated by the rapid fire, cross indexed, computerized, automated mood of modern living, it is refreshing to be reminded of the "silence of real communion"—the need and place of contemplation. Although the book does not purport to be written for those whose vocation is to prolonged contemplation, it convincingly describes to both the initiated and the novice the role of silent prayer in the

Christian scale of values. To the layman who seeks the consolations of contemplation the book will be a precious aid.

The Archbishop reminds us of another truth well known but again sometimes less deeply appreciated in an age that finds impatience the daily fare, that of the need for firm, abiding faith and deep soul-stirring constancy in our prayer. The "need to turn to God wholeheartedly" is no more an original discovery of Archbishop Bloom than it was of St. Theresa, St. Bernard or St. John of the Cross, but it is timely to have it pointed out again in cogent yet gentle language for our generation.

Mindful of the renewed ecumenical conversation and sympathy among the Christian traditions, it is pleasant and profitable to read the words of an Orthodox prelate prepared to share with us the rich resources of the Eastern heritage of prayer. In ways more profound than the phrase usually means, the Orthodox prelate's book meets a real need.

Our needs are so great because our deficiencies are so many. Our prayer is so constant because our dependence is so total. Archbishop Bloom's book, by presenting with pastoral simplicity and priestly concern the place of prayer in the daily concerns of modern Christians, does a great service to us all.

† John Wright
Bishop of Pittsburgh

September, 1967

FOREWORD*

Worship to me means a relationship. I used not to be a believer, then one day I discovered God and immediately he appeared to me to be the supreme value and the total meaning of life, but at the same time a person. I think that worship can mean nothing at all to someone for whom there is no object of worship. You cannot teach worship to someone who has not got a sense of the living God; you can teach him to act as if he believed, but it will not be the spontaneous attitude which is real worship. Therefore, as a foreword to this book on prayer, what I would like to convey is my certitude in the personal reality of a God with whom a relationship can be established. Then I would ask my reader to treat God as a neighbour, as someone, and value this knowledge in the same terms in which he values a relationship with a brother or a friend. This, I think, is essential.

One of the reasons why communal worship or private prayer seem to be so dead or so conventional is that the act of worship, which takes place in the heart communing with God, is too often missing. Every expression, either verbal or in action, may help, but they are only expressions of what is essential, namely, a deep silence of communion.

We all know in human relationships that love and friendship are deep when we can be silent with someone. As

* Adaptation of a talk given on the BBC in the 'Ten to Eight' programme first broadcast in 1965.

long as we need to talk in order to keep in touch, we can safely and sadly assume that the relationship is still superficial; and so, if we want to worship God, we must first of all learn to feel happy, being silent together with him. This is an easier thing to do than one might think at first; it needs a little time, some confidence and the courage to start.

Once the Curé d'Ars, a French saint of the eighteenth century, asked an old peasant what he was doing sitting for hours in the church, seemingly not even praying; the peasant replied: 'I look at him, he looks at me and we are happy together.' That man had learned to speak to God without breaking the silence of intimacy by words. If we can do that we can use any form of worship. If we try to make worship itself out of the words we use, we will get desperately tired of those words, because unless they have the depth of silence, they are shallow and tiresome.

But how inspiring words can be once they are backed by silence and are infused with the right spirit:

'O Lord, open Thou my lips; and my mouth shall show forth thy praise' (Ps 51:15).

I

The Essence of Prayer

THE GOSPEL OF St Matthew confronts us almost from the beginning with the very essence of prayer. The Magi saw the long-expected star, they set out without delay to find the king; they arrived at the manger, they knelt, they worshipped and they presented their gifts: they expressed prayer in its perfection, which is contemplation and adoration.

Often, in more or less popular literature about prayer, we are told that prayer is an enthralling adventure. It is a commonplace to hear: 'Come on, learn to pray; prayer is so interesting, so thrilling, it is the discovery of a new world; you will meet God, you will find the way to a spiritual life.' In a sense of course this is true; but something very much more far-reaching is being forgotten when such statements are made: it is that prayer is a dangerous adventure and that we cannot enter upon it without risk. As St Paul says, it is a fearful thing to fall into the hands of the living God (Heb 10:31). Therefore to set out deliberately to confront the living God is a dread adventure: every meeting with God is, in a certain sense, a last judgement. Whenever we

come into the presence of God, whether in the sacraments or in prayer, we are doing something which is full
of danger because, according to the words of scripture, God
is a fire. Unless we are ready to surrender ourselves without
reservation to the divine fire and to become that burning
bush of the desert, which burned but was never consumed,
we shall be scorched, because the experience of prayer can
only be known from the inside, and is not to be dallied with.

Coming nearer to God is always a discovery both of the
beauty of God and of the distance there is between him
and us. 'Distance' is an inadequate word, because it is not
determined by the fact that God is holy and that we are
sinful. Distance is determined by the attitude of the sinner
to God. We can approach God only if we do so with a
sense of coming to judgement. If we come having con-
demned ourselves; if we come because we love him in
spite of the fact that we are unfaithful, if we come to him,
loving him more than a godless security, then we are open
to him and he is open to us, and there is no distance; the
Lord comes close to us in an act of compassionate love.
But if we stand before God wrapped in our pride, in our
assertiveness, if we stand before him as though we had a
right to stand there, if we stand and question him, the distance that separates the creature and the creator becomes
infinite. There is a passage in the *Screwtape Letters* in which
C. S. Lewis suggests that distance, in this sense, is a relative
thing: when the great archangel came before God to
question him, the moment he asked his question, not in
order to understand in humility but in order to compel
God to give account, he found himself at an infinite distance from God. God had not moved, nor had Satan, and

yet without any motion, they were infinitely far apart (Letter XIX).

Whenever we approach God the contrast that exists between what he is and what we are becomes dreadfully clear. We may not be aware of this as long as we live at a distance from God, so to speak, as long as his presence or his image is dimmed in our thoughts and in our perceptions; but the nearer we come to God, the sharper the contrast appears. It is not the constant thought of their sins, but the vision of the holiness of God that makes the saints aware of their own sinfulness. When we consider ourselves without the fragrant background of God's presence, sins and virtues become small and somewhat irrelevant matters; it is against the background of the divine presence that they stand out in full relief and acquire their depth and tragedy.

Every time we come near God, it is either life or death we are confronted with. It is life if we come to him in the right spirit, and are renewed by him. It is death if we come to him without the spirit of worship and a contrite heart; it is death if we bring pride or arrogance. Therefore, before we set out on the so-called thrilling adventure of prayer, it cannot be too strongly stated that nothing more significant, more awe-inspiring, can occur than meeting the God we set out to meet. It is essential to realise that we will lose our life in the process: the old Adam we are must die. We are intensely attached to the old man, afraid for him, and it is very difficult, not only at the outset but years after we have begun, to feel that we are completely on the side of Christ, against the old Adam.

Prayer is an adventure which brings not a thrill but new responsibilities: as long as we are ignorant, nothing is asked of us, but as soon as we know anything, we are answerable for the use we make of that knowledge. It may be a gift, but we are responsible for any particle of truth we have acquired; as it becomes our own, we cannot leave it dormant but have to take it into account in our behaviour, and in this sense we are to answer for any truth we have understood.

It is only with a feeling of fear, of adoration, with the utmost veneration that we can approach this adventure of prayer, and we must live up to it outwardly as completely and precisely as possible. It is not enough to lounge in an armchair, saying: now, I place myself in an act of veneration in the presence of God. We have to realise that if Christ were standing in front of us, we would comport ourselves differently, and we must learn to behave in the presence of the invisible Lord as we would in the presence of the Lord made visible to us.

This implies primarily an attitude of mind and then its reflection upon the body. If Christ was there, before us, and we stood completely transparent to his gaze, in mind as well as in body, we would feel reverence, the fear of God, adoration, or else perhaps terror, but we should not be so easy in our behaviour as we are. The modern world has to a great extent lost the sense of prayer and physical attitudes have become secondary in people's minds, although they are anything but secondary. We forget that we are not a soul dwelling in a body, but a human being, made up of body and soul, and that we are called, according to St Paul, to glorify God in our spirit and in our body; our bodies as well as our souls are to be called to the glory of the kingdom of God (I Cor 6:20).

Too often prayer has no such importance in our lives that everything else fades away to give it room. Prayer is additional to a great many things; we wish God to be present, not because there is no life without him, not because he is the supreme value, but because it would be so nice, in addition to all the great benefits of God, to have also his presence. He is additional to our needs, and when we seek him in that spirit we do not meet him. Yet notwithstanding all that has just been said, prayer, dangerous as it appears, is the best way to go ahead towards the fulfilment of our calling, to become fully human, which means in full communion with God and, ultimately, what St Peter calls partakers of the divine nature.

Love and friendship do not grow if we are not prepared to sacrifice a great deal for their sake, and in the same way we must be ready to put aside many things in order to give God the first place.

'Thou shalt love the Lord thy God with all thy heart, and with all thy soul, and with all thy strength, and with all thy mind' (Lk 10:27). This seems to be a very simple command, and yet those words contain much more than one sees at a first glance. We all know what it is to love someone with all one's heart; we know the pleasure, not only of meeting but even of thinking of the beloved, the warm comfort it gives. It is in that way that we should try to love God, and whenever his name is mentioned, it should fill our heart and soul with infinite warmth. God should be at all times in our mind, whereas in fact we think of him only occasionally.

As for loving God with all our strength, we can only do it if we cast off deliberately everything that is not God's in us; by an effort of will we must turn ourselves constantly towards God, whether in prayer, which is easier, because in prayer we are already centred on God, or in action, which requires training, because in our actions we are concentrated on some material achievement and have to dedicate it to God by a special effort.

The Wise Men travelled a long way and nobody knows the difficulties they had to overcome. Each of us also travels as they did. They were loaded with gifts, gold for the king, frankincense for the God, myrrh for the man who was to suffer death. Where can we get gold, frankincense and myrrh, we who are indebted for everything to God? We know that everything we possess has been given us by God and is not even ours for ever or with certainty. Everything can be taken away from us except love, and this is what makes love unique and something we can give. Everything else, our limbs, our intelligence, our possessions can be taken by force from us, but with regard to love, there is no means of getting it, unless we give it. In that sense we are free with regard to loving, in a way in which we are not free in other activities of soul or body. Although fundamentally even love is a gift of God, because we cannot produce it out of ourselves, yet, once we possess it, it is the only thing that we can withold or offer.

Bernanos says in the *Diary of a Country Priest* that we can also offer our pride to God, 'Give your pride with all the rest, give everything.' Pride offered in that context becomes a gift of love, and everything which is a gift of love is well pleasing to God.

'Love your enemies, bless them that hate you' (Mt 5:44), is a command that may be more or less easy to follow; but to forgive those who inflict suffering on one's beloved is altogether different, and it makes people feel as if taken in disloyalty. Yet, the greater our love for the one who suffers, the greater our ability to share and to forgive, and in that sense the greatest love is achieved when one can say with Rabbi Yehel Mikhael 'I am my beloved'. As long as we say 'I' and 'he' we do not share the suffering and we cannot accept it. The mother of God at the foot of the cross was not in tears, as shown so often in western paintings; she was so completely in communion with her son that she had nothing to protest against. She was going through the crucifixion, together with Christ; she was going through her own death. The mother was fulfilling now what she had begun on the day of the presentation of Christ to the temple, when she had given her son. Alone of all the children of Israel he had been accepted as a sacrifice of blood. And she, who had brought him then, was now accepting the consequence of her ritual gesture which was finding fulfilment in reality. As he was then in communion with her, she was completely in communion with him now and she had nothing to protest against.

It is love that makes us one with the object of our love and makes it possible for us to share unreservedly, not only the suffering but also the attitude towards suffering and the executioner. We cannot imagine the mother of God or John the disciple protesting against what was the explicit will of the son of God crucified. 'No one is taking my life from me, I lay it down of myself' (Jn 10:18). He was dying willingly, of his own accord for the salvation of the world; his death was this salvation and therefore those who believed in him and wanted to be at one with him could share the suffering of his death, could undergo the passion together with him; but they could not reject it, they could not turn against the crowd that had crucified Christ, because this crucifixion was the will of Christ himself.

We can protest against someone's suffering, we can protest against someone's death, either when he himself, rightly or wrongly, takes a stand against it, or else when we do not share his intention and his attitude towards death and suffering; but then our love for that person is an incomplete love and creates separation. It is the kind of love shown by Peter when Christ, on the way to Jerusalem, told his disciples that he was going to his death; Peter 'took him and began to rebuke him', but Christ answered: 'Get thee behind me, Satan, for thou savourest not the things that be of God, but the things that be of men' (Mk 8:33). We can imagine that the wife of the thief on the left of Christ was full of the same protest against her husband's death as he himself was; in this respect there was complete communion between them, but they were sharing a wrong attitude.

But to share with Christ his passion, his crucifixion, his death, means to accept unreservedly all these events, in the same spirit as he did, that is, to accept them in an act of free will, to suffer together with the man of sorrows, to be there in silence, the very silence of Christ, interrupted only by a few decisive words, the silence of real communion; not just the silence of pity, but of compassion, which allows us to grow into complete oneness with the other so that there is no longer one and the other, but only one life and one death.

On many occasions throughout history people witnessed

persecution and were not afraid, but shared in the suffering and did not protest; for instance, Sophia, the mother who stood by each of her daughters, Faith, Hope and Charity, encouraging them to die, or many other martyrs who helped one another but never turned against the tormentors. The spirit of martyrdom can be brought out by several examples. The first expresses the spirit of martyrdom in itself, its basic attitude: a spirit of love which cannot be defeated by suffering or injustice. A very young priest, who was imprisoned at the beginning of the Russian revolution, and came out a broken man, was asked what was left of him, and he answered: 'Nothing is left of me, they have burnt out every single thing, love only survives.' A man who can say that has the right attitude and anyone who shares his tragedy must also share in his unshakeable love.

There is the example of a man who came back from Buchenwald and, when asked about himself, said that his sufferings were nothing compared to his broken-heartedness about those poor German youths who could be so cruel, and that thinking about the state of their souls, he could find no peace. His concern was not for himself, and he had spent four years there, nor for the innumerable people who had suffered and died around him; but for the condition of the tormentors. Those who suffered were on the side of Christ, those who were cruel were not.

Thirdly, there is this prayer written in a concentration camp by a Jewish prisoner:

> Peace to all men of evil will! Let there be an end to all vengeance, to all demands for punishment and retribution . . . Crimes have surpassed all measure, they can no longer be grasped by human understanding. There are too many martyrs

B

... And so, weigh not their sufferings on the scales of thy justice, Lord, and lay not these sufferings to the torturors' charge to exact a terrible reckoning from them. Pay them back in a different way! Put down in favour of the executioners, the informers, the traitors and all men of evil will, the courage, the spiritual strength of the others, their humility, their lofty dignity, their constant inner striving and invincible hope, the smile that staunched the tears, their love, their ravaged, broken hearts that remained steadfast and confident in the face of death itself, yes, even at moments of the utmost weakness ... Let all this, O Lord, be laid before thee for the forgiveness of sins, as a ransom for the triumph of righteousness, let the good and not the evil be taken into account! And may we remain in our enemies' memory not as their victims, not as a nightmare, not as haunting spectres, but as helpers in their striving to destroy the fury of their criminal passions. There is nothing more that we want of them. And when it is all over, grant us to live among men as men, and may peace come again to our poor earth – peace for men of goodwill and for all the others ...*

There was also a Russian bishop who said that it is a privilege for a christian to die a martyr, because none but a martyr can, at the last judgement, take his stand in front of God's judgement seat and say, 'According to thy word and thy example, I have forgiven. Thou hast no claim against them any more.' Which means that the one who suffers martyrdom in Christ, whose love is not defeated by suffering, acquires unconditional power of forgiving over the one who has inflicted the suffering. And this can be applied on a much lower level, on the level of everyday life; anyone who suffers a minor injustice from someone else can forgive or refuse to forgive. But this is a two-edged

* Found in the archives of a German concentration camp and published in the Suddeutsche Zeitung.

sword; if you do not forgive, you will not be forgiven either.

French Roman Catholics, with their acute sense of justice and the honour of God, are very conscious of the victory which Christ can gain through the suffering of people: since 1797 there has existed an Order of Reparation, which by perpetual adoration of the Blessed Sacrament asks forgiveness for the crimes of the world and the forgiveness of individual sinners by their victim's prayers. This Order is also educational and aims to give children and adults the spirit of love.

Typical also is the story of the French general Maurice d'Elbée during the revolutionary wars; his men captured some *Bleus* and wanted to shoot them; the general, unwillingly, had to consent, but he insisted that they should first read the Lord's Prayer aloud, which they did, and when they came to the words 'Forgive us our trespasses as we forgive them that trespass against us', they understood, they wept and let the prisoners go. Later on, in 1794, General d'Elbée was himself shot by the *Bleus*.

Jean Daniélou, the French Jesuit writer, says in *Holy Pagans* that suffering is the link between the righteous and sinners, the righteous man who endures suffering and the sinner who inflicts it. If there were not that link, they would drift apart and sinners and righteous would remain on parallel lines that never meet. In that case, the righteous would have no power over the sinner because one cannot deal with what one does not meet.

II

The Lord's Prayer

———————————

ALTHOUGH IT IS very simple, and is used so constantly, The Lord's Prayer is a great problem and a difficult prayer; it is the only one which the Lord gave, yet, reading the Acts, one never finds it used by anyone at all, which is not what one would expect from the words that introduce the prayer in Luke 11:1, 'Lord, teach us to pray, as John also taught his disciples.' But not being quoted does not mean not being used, and in a way the Lord's Prayer is not only a prayer but a whole way of life expressed in the form of a prayer: it is the image of the gradual ascent of the soul from bondage to freedom. The prayer is built with striking precision. Just as when a pebble falls into a pond we can observe the ripples spreading from the place where the pebble fell, farther and farther towards the banks, or on the contrary, we may begin with the banks and work back to the source of the movement, in the same way the Lord's Prayer can be analysed either beginning with the first words, or else with the last. It is infinitely easier to begin the progression from the outside towards the centre of the prayer, although for Christ and for the Church it is the other way which is right.

This is a prayer of sonship – 'Our Father' – and in a certain sense, although it may be used by anyone who approaches the Lord, it expresses adequately only the relationship of those who are in the Church of God, who, in Christ, have found their way to their father, because it is only through Christ and in him that we become the sons of God.

This teaching of a spiritual life can best be understood when set in parallel with the story of Exodus and within the experience of the beatitudes. Starting with the last words of the prayer and moving towards the first, we see it as a way of ascent; our starting-point at the end defines a captivity, the last word at the beginning defines our state of sonship.

The people of God, who had come free to the land of Egypt, had gradually become enslaved. The conditions of their life brought home to them their state of slavery: work was heavier and heavier, the conditions of living more and more miserable; but this was not enough to make them move towards real freedom. If misery increases beyond a certain point, it may lead to rebellion, to violence, to attempted escape from the painful, unbearable situation; but essentially neither rebellion nor flight make us free, because freedom is first of all an inner situation with regard to God, to self and to the surrounding world.

Every time they attempted to leave the country, new and heavier tasks were given to the Jews. When they had to make bricks, they were refused the necessary straw, and Pharaoh said: 'Let them go and gather straw for themselves' (Ex 5:7), and 'Let more work be laid upon them, that they may labour therein.' He wanted them so

completely exhausted, so completely concerned with the toil
that they should have no thought for rebellion or deliverance any more. In the same way there is no hope for us
as long as we are enthralled by the prince of this world, the
devil, with all the powers at his disposal to enslave human
souls and bodies and keep them away from the living God.
Unless God comes himself to deliver us, there will be no
deliverance, but eternal slavery; and the first words we
find in the Lord's Prayer are for this very thing: 'Deliver
us from Evil.' Deliverance from evil is exactly what was
done in the land of Egypt through Moses, and what is
achieved at baptism by the power of God, given to his
Church. The word of God resounds in this world, calling
everyone to freedom, giving the hope that comes from
heaven to those who have lost their hope on earth. This
word of God is preached and resounds in the human soul,
making a man a learner of the Church, making him one
who stands as an outsider in the porch, one who has heard
the call and has come to listen (Rom 10:17).

When the learner is determined to become a free man in
the kingdom of the Lord, the Church undertakes certain
actions. What would be the good of asking a slave, who is
still in the power of his master, whether he wants to be
free? If he dares ask for the freedom which is offered, he
knows that he will be cruelly punished the moment he is
left alone again with his master. Through fear and from a
habit of slavery a man cannot ask for freedom until he is
delivered from the authority of the devil. Therefore, before
any question is asked of the one who stands there, with a
new hope in divine salvation, he is made free from the
power of Satan. This is the meaning of the exorcisms

which are read at the outset of the baptismal service both
in the Orthodox and Roman Catholic Churches. It is only
when a man is free from the bonds of slavery that he is
asked if he renounces the devil and if he wants to join
Christ. And only after a free answer does the Church
integrate him into herself, into the Body of Christ. The
devil wants slaves, but God wants free men in harmony of
will with him. The evil one in terms of Exodus was Egypt
and Pharaoh, and all the values attached to them, namely,
to be fed and kept alive, on condition that they were submissive slaves. And for us the act of prayer, which is a more
essential, final act of rebellion against slavery than taking
up arms, is at the same time a sort of return into our sense
of responsibility and relatedness to God.

So the first situation with which Exodus begins, and we
begin, is the discovery of slavery and that it cannot be
resolved by an act of rebellion or flight, because whether
we flee or whether we rebel we remain slaves, unless we
re-establish ourselves, with regard to God and to all the
situations of life, in the way taught by the first beatitude:
'Blessed are the poor in spirit, for theirs is the Kingdom of
Heaven.' In itself, poverty, the state of a slave, is no pass-
port to the kingdom of heaven; the slave can be deprived
not only of earthly goods but also of heavenly goods; such
poverty can be more overwhelming than simple deprivation of what we need for earthly life. St John Chrysostom
says that the poor man is not so much he who does not
possess, but he who wants what he does not possess.

Poverty is not rooted in what we have or have not, but
in the degree to which we long for what is out of reach.
When we think of our human condition we can discover

quite easily that we are utterly poor and destitute because whatever we possess is never ours, however rich and wealthy we seem to be. When we try to grasp anything we discover quite soon that it has gone. Our being is rooted in nothing except the sovereign creative word of God who called us out of total, radical absence into his presence. The life and health that we possess we cannot keep, and not only health but so many of our psychosomatic qualities: a man of great intelligence, because a minute vessel has burst in his head, becomes senile and is finished intellectually. In the realm of our feelings, for some accountable or unaccountable reason, say 'flu or tiredness, we cannot at the right moment, and at will, feel the sympathy for someone which we wish so much to feel, or we go to church and we are of stone. This is the basic poverty, but does it make us the children of the kingdom? It does not, because if at every moment of our life we feel in a state of misery, that all things escape us, if we are aware only of the fact that we do not possess them, it does not make us the joyful children of a kingdom of divine love, but the miserable victims of a situation over which we have no power and which we hate.

This brings us back to the words 'poor *in spirit*'; the poverty that opens the kingdom of heaven lies in the knowledge that if nothing that is mine is really mine, then everything that is mine is a gift of love, divine or human love, and that makes things quite different. If we realise that we have no being in ourselves, and yet we exist, we can say that there is a sustained unceasing act of divine love. If we see that whatever we have, we can in no wise compel to be ours, then everything is divine love, concretely expressed

at every single moment; and then poverty is the root of
perfect joy because all we have proves love. We should
never attempt to appropriate things to ourselves because
to call something 'ours', and not a constant gift of God,
means less and not more. If it is mine, it is alien to the
relationship of mutual love; if it is his and I possess it from
day to day, from split second to split second, it is a continu-
ously renewed act of divine love. Then we come to the
joyful thought: 'Thanks be to God, it is not mine; if it
were mine, it would mean possession, but alas without
love.' The relationship to which this thought brings us is
what the gospel calls the kingdom of God. Only those
belong to the kingdom who receive all things from the
king in the relationship of mutual love and who do not
want to be rich, because to be rich means to be dispossessed
of love while possessed of things. The moment when we
discover God within the situation and that all things are
God's and everything is of God, then we begin to enter
this divine kingdom and acquire freedom.

It was only when the Jews, guided and enlightened by
Moses, realised that their state of enslavement had something to do with God, and was not simply a man-made
situation, it was only when they turned to God, when they
re-established a relationship which is that of the kingdom,
that something could happen; and that is true for all of us,
because it is only when we realise that we are slaves, when
we realise that we are destitute, but when we also realise
that this happens within the divine wisdom and that all
things are within the divine power, that we can turn to
Him and say, 'Deliver us from the evil one.'

As the Jews were called by Moses to escape from the

country of Egypt, to follow him in the dark night, to cross the Red Sea, so also is each individual brought into the wilderness, where a new period begins. He is free, but not yet enjoying the glory of the promised land, because he has taken with him, out of the land of Egypt, the soul of a slave, the habits of a slave, the temptations of a slave; and the education of a free man takes infinitely more time than the discovery of his enslavement. The spirit of slavery remains very close, and its standards are still there and very potent: a slave has somewhere to rest his head, a slave is assured of food, a slave has a social standing, however low, he is secure because his master is responsible for him. So to be a slave, however painful, humiliating and distressing the situation, is also a form of security, while to become a free person is a state of utter insecurity; we take our destiny into our own hands and it is only when our freedom is rooted in God that we become secure in a new way, and a very different one.

This sense of insecurity is brought out in Samuel, when the Jews asked the prophet to give them a king. For centuries they had been led by God, that is by men who, being saints, knew God's ways; as Amos says (3:7), a prophet is one with whom God shares his thoughts. And then in the time of Samuel, the Jews discover that to be under God alone is, in a worldly sense, total insecurity because it depends on saintliness, on dedication, on moral values which are hard to get, and they turn to Samuel and ask him to give them a king, because 'We want to be like every other nation with the security which every nation has.'

Samuel does not want to agree to what he sees is an

apostasy; but God tells him 'Hearken to the voice of thy people . . . for they have not rejected thee, but they have rejected me, that I should not reign over them' (I Sam 8:9). And a whole picture follows of what their life will be: 'This will be the manner of the king that shall reign over you: he will take your sons, and appoint them for himself, for his chariots, and to be his horsemen; and some shall run before his chariots . . . And he will take your daughters to be confectionaries, and to be cooks and to be bakers.' 'Nevertheless the people refused to obey the voice of Samuel and they said, Nay; but we will have a king over us' (I Sam 8:19). They want to buy security at the cost of freedom. It is not what God wills for us, and what happens is exactly the reverse of the events of Exodus: God's will is that the security of slaves is to be forsaken and replaced by the insecurity of free men in the making. This is a difficult situation because while we are in the making we do not yet know how to be free and we do not want to be slaves any more. Remember what happened to the Jews in the wilderness, how often they regretted the time when they were enslaved in Egypt, but fed. How often they complained that now they were without a roof, without food, dependent on the will of God, which they had not yet learned to rely upon completely; for God gives us grace, but leaves it to us to become new creatures.

Like the Jews in Egypt we have spent all our lives as slaves; we are not yet in our souls, in our wills, in our whole selves, real free men: left to our own powers we may fall into temptation. And these words 'Lead us not into temptation' – submit us not to the severe test – must remind us of the forty years the Jews spent crossing the short expanse of territory between the land of Egypt and the promised land. They took so long because whenever they turned away from God, their path turned away from the promised land. The only way in which we can reach the promised land is to follow in the steps of the Lord. Whenever our heart turns back to the land of Egypt, we retrace our steps, we go astray. We have all been set free by the mercy of God, we are all on our way, but who will say that he does not retrace his steps constantly, or turn from the right path? 'Lead us not into temptation', let us not fall back into our state of slavery.

Once we have become aware of our enslavement, and have passed from mere lamentation and a sense of misery into a sense of brokenheartedness and poverty of spirit, our imprisonment in the land of Egypt is answered by the words of the next beatitudes: 'Blessed are they that mourn, for they shall be comforted', 'Blessed are the meek, for they shall inherit the earth'. This mourning that is the result of the discovery of the kingdom, of one's own responsibility, of the tragedy of being a slave, is a more bitter mourning than that which is the lot of the simple slave. The slave complains about an outer situation; this mourner, who is blessed by God, does not complain, he is brokenhearted, and he is aware that his outer enslavement is the expression of something far more tragic: his inner enslavement, his severance from the closeness of God. And nothing can be done to escape this situation unless meekness is attained.

Meekness is a difficult word which has acquired various connotations and since it is extremely rare in practice, we cannot turn to our experience of meek people, which would give us a clue to the meaning of the word. We find in J. B. Phillips' translation: 'Happy are those who claim nothing', meaning 'Blessed are those who do not try to possess'. The moment you do not want to possess, you become free because, whatever you do possess, by that you are possessed. Another interpretation of the word meek is found in the translation of the Greek word into a slavonic word meaning 'made tame'. A person or an animal that has been tamed is not simply terrified of punishment and subject to the authority of the master; it is someone in whom the process has gone farther, someone who has acquired a new quality and who by this tameness escapes the violence of coercion.

At the threshold of our salvation from the slavery of Egypt stands the condition that we should be tamed; in other words, that we should recognise in the situation in which we are, depth, significance, the presence of the divine will, and it should be neither flight nor rebellion, but a movement guided by God, which begins with the kingdom of heaven that is within us and develops into the kingdom on earth. It is a period of wavering and of inner struggle: 'Lead us not into temptation O Lord, Protect us in the trial, help us in the fight which has begun for us.' And now we are at the point when a move can be made. Look back at Exodus, at the Jews' awareness that they are not simply slaves but the people of God that had become enslaved because of their moral weaknesses. They had to take risks, because no one is ever freed by a slave owner, and they had to cross the Red Sea; but beyond the Red Sea it was not yet the promised land, it was the burning desert and they were aware of it and knew that they would have to cross it in the face of great difficulties. And so are we when we decide to make a move that will liberate us from our enslavement: we must be aware that we shall be attacked by violence, by beguilement, by the inner enemies that are our old habits, our old craving for security, and that nothing is promised us, except the desert beyond. Beyond that is the promised land, but far beyond, and we must accept the risks of the journey.

There is one thing that stands as a line of demarcation between Egypt and the desert, between slavery and freedom; it is a moment when we act decisively and become new people, establishing ourselves in an absolutely new moral situation. In terms of geography it was the Red Sea, in terms of the Lord's Prayer it is 'Forgive us our trespasses as we forgive'. This 'as we forgive' is the moment when we take our salvation into our own hands, because whatever God does depends on what we do; and this is tremendously important in terms of ordinary life. If these people who are moving out of Egypt into the promised land take with them, out of the Land of Egypt, their fears, their resentments, their hatreds, their grievances, they will be slaves in the promised land. They will not be freemen, even in the making. And this is why at the demarcation line between the trials of fire and the beguilement of old habits, stands this absolute condition which God never relaxes: as you forgive, the measure which you use will be used for you; and as you forgive, you will be forgiven; what you do not forgive will be held against you. It is not that God does not want to forgive, but if we come unforgiving, we check the mystery of love, we refuse it and there is no place for us in the kingdom. We cannot go farther if we are not forgiven, and we cannot be forgiven as long as we have not forgiven everyone of those who have wronged us. This is quite sharp and real and precise and no one has any right to imagine that he is in the kingdom of God, that he belongs to it, if there is still unforgiveness in his heart. To forgive one's enemies is the first, the most elementary characteristic of a christian; failing this, we are not yet christian at all, but are still wandering in the scorching wilderness of Sinai.

But forgiveness is something extremely difficult to achieve. To grant forgiveness at a moment of softening of the heart, in an emotional crisis is comparatively easy; not to take it back is something that hardly anyone knows how to do. What we call forgiveness is often putting the other one on probation, nothing more; and lucky are the forgiven people if it is only probation and not remand. We wait impatiently for evidence of repentance, we want to be sure that the penitent is not the same any more, but this situation can last a lifetime and our attitude is exactly the contrary of everything which the gospel teaches, and indeed commands us, to do. So the law of forgiveness is not a little brook on the boundary between slavery and freedom: it has breadth and depth, it is the Red Sea. The Jews did not get over it by their own effort in man-made boats, the Red Sea was cut open by the power of God; God had to lead them across. But to be led by God one must commune with this quality of God which is the ability to forgive. God remembers, in the sense that, once we have done wrong, he will for ever, until we change, take into account that we are weak and frail; but he will never remember in terms of accusation or condemnation; it will never be brought up against us. The Lord will yoke himself together with us, into our lives, and he will have more weight to carry, he will have a heavier cross, a new ascent to Calvary which we are unwilling or incapable of undertaking.

To be able to say the first sentence that we have discussed – 'Deliver us from the evil one' – requires such a reassessment of values and such a new attitude that we can hardly begin to say it otherwise than in a cry, which is as yet unsubstantiated by an inner change in us. We feel a longing which is not yet capable of achievement; to ask God to protect us in the trial is to ask for a radical change in our situation. But to be able to say 'Forgive as I forgive' is even more difficult; it is one of the greatest problems of life. Thus, if you are not prepared to leave behind you every resentment that you have against those who were your overlords or slavedrivers, you cannot cross. If you are capable of forgiving, that is of leaving behind in the land of slavery, all your slavish mentality, all your greed and grasping and bitterness, you can cross. After that you are in the scorching wilderness, because it will take time for a free man to be made out of a slave.

All that we possessed as slaves in the land of Egypt we are deprived of – no roof, no shelter, no food, nothing but the wilderness and God. Earth is no longer capable of feeding us; we can no longer rely on natural food, so we pray 'give us day by day our daily bread'. God gives it even when we go astray, because if he did not we should die before we could reach the border of the promised land. Keep us alive, O God, give us time to err, to repent, to take the right course.

'Our daily bread' is one of the possible ways of translating the Greek text. This bread, which in Greek is called *epiousion*, may be daily, but it may also be the bread that is beyond substance. The Fathers of the Church, beginning with Origen and Tertullian, have always interpreted this passage as referring not only to our human needs but also to the mysterious bread of the eucharist. Unless we are fed in this new way, mysteriously, by divine bread (because we depend now for our existence on God alone) we will not survive (Jn 6:53). God sent to his people the manna and gave them water from the rock, struck by the rod of Moses. The two gifts are images of Christ: 'Man shall not live by bread alone but by every word that proceedeth from the mouth of God.' This is what Christ recalled from the Old Testament (Dt 8:3) to confound Satan. This 'word' is not simply words but first of all the Word that resounds for ever, upholding all things created, and then also the Word incarnate, Jesus of Nazareth; furthermore, it is the bread of which manna was the image, the bread which we receive in communion. The waters that ran and filled the brooks and the rivers at the command of Moses, are the image of that water which was promised to the Samaritan woman and of the blood of Christ which is our life.

Exodus is a complex image in terms of the Lord's Prayer; in the beatitudes we find the same progression: 'Blessed are they which do hunger and thirst after righteousness, for they shall be filled', 'Blessed are the merciful, for they shall obtain mercy'. First a simple bodily hunger and thirst, a deprivation of all possessions, which were a gift of corruption, a gift of the earth from the overlord, a stamp of slavery, and then exactly in the way in which the mourning

c

of the second beatitude is increased, the moment we are turned Godwards, so this thirst and hunger are turned towards righteousness. A new dimension has been disclosed to men, one of longing, of craving, a dimension which is defined in one of the secret prayers in the liturgy as 'The Kingdom for to come', when we thank God that he has given us his kingdom for which we are longing. In the liturgy the kingdom is there, but in the journey through the desert it is ahead, in a germinal state, still beyond reach. It is within us, as an attitude, as a relationship, but certainly not as something which is already life, on which we can feed and by which we can be kept alive. There is the bodily hunger, born of our past and of our present, and the spiritual hunger, born of our future and of our vocation.

'Blessed are the merciful.' This journey is not a lonely one; in terms of Exodus it was the whole people of God who were launched out, side by side, as a unit; in terms of the Lord's Prayer and our vocation, it is the Church, it is mankind, it is everyone who is on this journey; and there is one thing of immense importance that we must learn, namely, mercy for our brothers who are journeying together with us. Unless we are willing to bear one another's burdens, to carry one another's weight, to receive one another as Christ receives us, in mercy, there is no way across the wilderness. This journey in the scorching heat, in the thirst and hunger, in the exertion of becoming a new man, is a time of mercy, of mutual charity; otherwise none will come to the place where God's law is proclaimed, where the tables of the law are offered. Thirst for righteousness and fulfilment goes hand in hand with mercy for the companions who walk side by side through the heat and the sufferings; and this thirst and hunger imply more, now, than just absence of food. When the Jews arrive one day at the foot of Sinai, they are capable of understanding and of being; they have been tamed and have become one people with one consciousness, with one direction, one intention. They are God's people, in motion towards the promised land. Their hearts that were darkened have become more transluscent, more pure. At the foot of the mountain it will be given them, to each according to his strength and capabilities, to see something of God (because 'Blessed are the pure in heart, for they shall see God'), to each of them in a different way, exactly as the disciples saw Christ transfigured on Mount Tabor, according to what they could comprehend.

At this point a new tragedy occurs: Moses discovers that the Jews have betrayed their vocation and he breaks the tables of the law; those which are afterwards given are the same, yet not the same: the difference is perhaps shown in the fact that when Moses brought the law the second time, he had a shining on his face which no one could bear (Ex 34:30); neither could they bear the Lord revealed in all his glory and fragrance. What they are given is what they can bear, but it is a law written by Moses (Ex 34:27) and not simply a divine revelation of love, 'written by the finger of God' (Ex 31:18). The law stands half way between lawlessness and grace; one can trace three steps in striking progression: in Genesis we see the violent Lamech, who says that if he is offended he will avenge himself seventy and seven fold (Gn 4:24); when we come to Sinai, we are told, an eye for an eye and a tooth for a tooth; and when we hear Christ, we are told 'seventy times seven shalt thou forgive thy brother'. These are the measures of human revolt against equity and against grace.

Khomiakov, a Russian theologian of the nineteenth century, says that the will of God is a curse for the demons, law for the servants of God and freedom for the children of God. This seems so true when we examine the gradual progression of the Jews from Egypt to the promised land. They departed slaves, who had just become aware of their potentialities as prospective children of God; they had to outgrow the mentality of slaves and attain the spirit and stature of sons; this took place gradually in the course of a long and extremely painful process. We see them slowly being built into a community of servants of God, of people who recognised that their Lord was no longer Pharaoh but the Lord of Hosts, to whom they acknowledged that they owed allegiance and unconditional obedience; they could expect from him both punishment and reward, knowing that he was leading them beyond what they then knew, into something which was their final vocation.

It is a very common thought in the writings of the early christian ascetics that man must go through these three stages – slave, hireling and son. The slave is one who obeys for fear, the hireling is one who obeys for reward and the son is one who acts for love. We can see in Exodus how gradually the people of God had become more than slaves and hirelings and the law stands at the threshold, geographically speaking, of the promised land.

At this threshold they discover, each with the ability that is his, with the depth of spirit that is his, God's own will, God's own mind, for this law can be seen in several ways: if we take it formally, sentence by sentence, it is a series of commandments: 'Thou shalt, thou shalt not,' in that sense it is law in the mentality of the Old Testament. But on the other hand, if we look at it with the eyes of the New Testament, with the eyes of our human vocation, as an increasing number were able to look at this law in the course of time after Exodus, we see that these various commandments, these imperatives, coalesce into two commandments: the love of God and the love of man. The first four of the ten are the love of God expressed concretely; and in the six other commandments we have the love of man, also made concrete, tangible, workable. The law is discipline and rule for those who are still in the making, who are still in the process of becoming sons, but at the same time it is already the law of the New Testament. The problem between man and man and between man and God is that of establishing divine peace, peace in the name of God, peace which is not built on mutual attraction or sympathy, but which is built on more basic facts; our common sonship, our common Lord, our human solidarity and our narrower church solidarity. Divine and human love must be summed up first of all in the establishment of the right relationships, the right relationship with God, with men and also with one's self.

We have seen that to exist in the desert, the absolute prerequisite is mutual forgiveness, now another step must be taken; whereas we find in Exodus the imperative law which expresses the mind and will of God, we find in the Lord's Prayer 'Thy will be done'. 'Thy will be done' is not a submissive readiness to bear God's will, as we often take it to be. It is the positive attitude of those who have gone through the wilderness, who have entered the promised land and who set out to make the will of God present and real on earth as it is in heaven. St Paul says that we are a colony of heaven (Phil 3:20; Moffat's translation). He means a group of people whose mother city is heaven, who are on earth to conquer it for God and to bring the kingdom of God if only to a small spot. It is a peculiar type of conquest, which consists in winning over people to the realm of peace, making them subject to the prince of peace and making them enter into the harmony which we call the kingdom of God. It is indeed a conquest, a peacemaking that will make us sheep among wolves, seeds scattered by the sower, which must die in order to bear fruit and to feed others.

'Thy will be done' seen in this way from within our situation as sons is something quite different from the kind of obedience, submissive or resistant, which we have seen in the beginning of Exodus, when Moses tried to put his countrymen in motion towards freedom. Now they have, we have, the mind of Christ, now we know the will of God, we are no longer servants but friends (Jn 15:15). He does not mean a vague relationship of goodwill, but something extremely deep that binds us together. This is the situation in which we walk into the promised land, when we say in a new way 'Thy will be done', not as an alien will, not as a will strong and able to break us, but as a will with which we have become completely harmonious. And we must, the moment we do this, accept all that is implied in being sons of God, in being members of the one body. As he came into the world to die for the salvation of the world, so are we elect for this purpose; and it may be at the cost of our own lives that we are to bring peace around us and establish the kingdom.

There is a difference between God the king, perceived in the land of Egypt, or in the scorching wilderness, and in the new situation of the promised land. First, his will would prevail anyhow, whatever resistance one opposed to it would be broken: obedience means subjection. Secondly, a gradual training shows that this king is not an overlord, a slavedriver, but a king of goodwill, and that obedience to him transforms all; that we can be not just subjects but his own people, his army in motion. Lastly, we discover the king in the full sense of this word as summed up by St Basil: 'Every ruler can rule, only a king can die for his subjects.' There is here such identification of the king with his subjects, that is with his kingdom, that whatever happens to the kingdom happens to the king; and not only identification, but an act of substitutive love which makes the king take the place of his subjects. The king becomes man, God is incarnate. He enters into the historical destiny of mankind, he puts on the flesh that makes him part and parcel of the total cosmos, with its tragedy caused by the human fall. He goes to the very depth of human condition, up to judgement, iniquitous condemnation and death, the experience of having lost God and so being able to die. The kingdom of which we speak in this petition is the kingdom of this king. If we are not at one with him and with all the spirit of the kingdom, now understood in a new way, we are not capable of being called the children of God, or of saying 'Thy Kingdom come'. But what we must realise is that the kingdom we ask for is a kingdom which is defined by the last beatitudes: 'Blessed are they which are persecuted.' 'Blessed are ye, when men shall revile you, and persecute you and shall say all manner of evil against you, for my sake.' If the kingdom is to come, we are to pay the cost which is defined in these beatitudes. The kingdom of which we are speaking is a kingdom of love and it would be superficially, seemingly, so nice to enter it; yet it is not nice, because love has got a tragic side, it means death to each of us, the complete dying out of our selfish, self-centred self, and not dying out as a flower fades away but dying a cruel death, the death of the crucifixion.

Only within the situation of the kingdom can the Name of God be hallowed and receive glory from us; because it is not our words and our gestures, even liturgical, that give glory to the name of God, it is our being the kingdom, which is the radiance and the glory of our maker and our saviour. And this name is love, one God in the Trinity.

As we see it now, the Lord's Prayer has a complete universal value and significance, expressing, though in reverse order, the ascent of every soul, from the captivity of sin to the plenitude of life in God; it is not just a prayer, it is *the* prayer of christians. The first words 'Our Father' are characteristically christian. In St Matthew 11:27 the Lord says: 'No man knoweth the Son but the Father, neither knoweth any man the Father, save the Son and he to whomsoever the Son will reveal him.' To know God as our father in an approximate way is given not only to christians but to many people, yet to know him as our father in the way in which Christ revealed it to us, is given only to christians in Christ. Outside the biblical revelation God appears to us as the creator of all things. A life attentive and worshipful may teach us that this creator is merciful, loving, full of wisdom, and by analogy may lead us to speak of the creator of all things in terms of fatherhood; he deals with us in the way in which a father deals with his children.

Even before the revelation of Christ we find in scripture one striking example of a man who was strictly speaking a pagan, but was on the verge of this knowledge of God in terms of sonship and fatherhood; it is Job. He is termed a pagan because he does not belong to the race of Abraham, he is not one of the inheritors of the promises to Abraham. He is one of the most striking figures of the Old Testament because of his contest with God. The three men who argue with him know God as their overlord: God is entitled to do what he has done to Job, God is right in whatever he does because he is the Lord of all things. And that is just the point which Job cannot accept, because he knows God differently. In his spiritual experience he knows already that God is not simply the overlord that is above all. He cannot accept him as one wielding arbitrary power, as an almighty being who can and has a right to do anything he chooses. Since, however, God has not yet said anything about himself, all this is a hope, a prophetic vision and not yet the very revelation of God in his fatherhood.

When the Lord appears to Job and answers his questions, he speaks in terms of the pagan revelation, which is typified by the words of the Psalm: 'The heavens declare the glory of God and the firmament sheweth his handywork' (Ps 19:1). Job understands, because, as Paul says, repeating Jeremiah (31:33), 'The Law of God is written in our hearts' (Rom 2:15). God confronts Job with a vision of all the created world and reasons with him; then, in spite of the fact that Job is apparently found wrong, God declares that he is more right than his gainsayers, than those who regard God as an earthly overlord. Although he fell short of a real knowledge of the divine fatherhood he had gone beyond what his friends knew about God. One may say that in the Old Testament we find in Job the first prophetic vision of the fatherhood of God and of that salvation of mankind that can be achieved only by someone who is the equal of both God and man. When Job turns accusingly towards God, and says, 'Neither is there any daysman (mediator) betwixt us, that might lay his hand upon us both' (Job 9:33), we see in him one who has outgrown the understanding of his contemporaries, but who has as yet no ground to affirm his faith and his knowledge, because God has not yet spoken through Christ.

The mystery of sonship and the mystery of fatherhood are correlative: you cannot know the father, unless you know the son, neither can you know the son, unless you are the father; there is no knowledge from without. Our relationship with God is based on an act of faith, supplemented by God's response, that brings this act of faith to fruition. The way in which we become members of Christ is an act of faith, fulfilled by God in baptism. In a way which is known only to God and to those who have been called and renewed, we become, by participation, what Christ is by birth. It is only by becoming members of Christ that we become sons of God. What we must not forget is that the fatherhood of God is more than an attitude of warmth and affection, it is more real and more sharply true: God becomes in Christ, the father of those who become members of the body of Christ, but one does not get linked with Christ by any kind of loose sentimentality: it is an ascetical effort which may take a lifetime and cost far more than one guessed at the start.

The fact that Christ and we become one, means that what applies to Christ applies to us, and that we can, in a way unknown to the rest of the world, call God our father, no longer by analogy, no longer in terms of anticipation or prophecy, but in terms of Christ. This has a direct bearing upon the Lord's Prayer: on the one hand, the prayer can be used by anyone, because it is universal, it is the ladder of our ascent towards God, on the other hand, it is absolutely particular and exclusive: it is the prayer of those who are, in Christ, the sons of the eternal father, who can speak to him as sons.

When the prayer is envisaged in its universal meaning, it is safer to study and analyse it in terms of an ascent, but it is not the way in which Christ has given it to those who, in him and together with him, are the children of God, because for them it is no longer an ascent that is spoken of, it is a state, a situation; we are, in the Church, the children of God, and these first words 'Our Father' establish the fact and make us take our stand where we belong. It is no good saying we are unworthy of this calling. We have accepted it, and it is ours. We may be the prodigal son and we will have to answer for it, but what is certain is that nothing can transform us back into that which we no longer are. When the prodigal son returned to his father, and was about to say: 'I am no more worthy to be called thy son, make me as one of thy hired servants' (Lk 15:19), the father allowed him to pronounce the first words: 'I have sinned against heaven and in thy sight and am no more worthy to be called thy son', but there he stopped him. Yes, he is not worthy, but he is a son in spite of his unworthiness. You cannot cease to be a member of your family, whatever you do, whether worthy or not. Whatever we are, whatever our life is, however unworthy we we are to be called the sons of God, or to call God our father, we have no escape. That is where we stand. He is our father, and we are answerable for the relationship of sonship. We are created by him as his children and it is only by rejecting our birthright that we become prodigal sons. Imagine that the prodigal son did not come back, but settled and married in the strange land, the child born of this marriage would be organically related to the prodigal's father. If he went back to his father's native land he would be received as one of the family; if he did not go back he would be answerable for not returning and choosing to remain a stranger to his father's family.

It is baptism which is the return of the children of many generations to the household of the father. And we baptise a child in the same spirit in which we cure a baby born with a disease. If later on he wrongly comes to think that it would have been more convenient to have kept his infirmity, to be of no use to society and to be free from the burden of social obligations, that is another matter. The Church, in baptising a child, heals it in order to make it a responsible member of the only real society.

Rejection of one's baptism amounts to the rejection of an act of healing. In baptism we not only become healthy but we become organically members of the body of Christ.

At that point, calling God 'Our Father' we have come

to Zion, to the top of the mount, and at the top of the mount we find the Father, divine love, the revelation of the Trinity; and just without the walls the small hill which we call Calvary, with history and eternity blending there in this vision. From there we can turn round and look back. This is where the christian should begin his christian life, having fulfilled this ascent, and should begin to say the Lord's Prayer in the order in which the Lord gives it to us as the prayer of the only begotten Son, the prayer of the Church, the prayer of each of us in our togetherness with all, as a person who is a son within the Son. And it is only then that we can go down from the top of the mountain, step by step, to meet those who are still on their way or those who have not yet begun their way.

III

The Prayer of Bartimaeus

THE CASE OF Bartimaeus, as recorded in Mark 10:46, gives us some insight into a certain number of points relating to prayer.

And they came to Jericho; and as he went out of Jericho with his disciples and a great number of people, blind Bartimaeus, the son of Timaeus, sat by the highway side, begging. And when he heard that it was Jesus of Nazareth, he began to cry out, and say, 'Jesus, thou son of David, have mercy upon me.' And many charged him that he should hold his peace; but he cried the more a great deal, 'Thou, son of David, have mercy on me.' And Jesus stood still, and commanded him to be called, and they called the blind man, saying to him, be of good comfort, rise; he calleth thee. And he, casting away his garment, rose, and came to Jesus. And Jesus answered and said unto him, 'What wilt thou that I should do unto thee?' The blind man said unto Him, 'Lord, that I might receive my sight.' And Jesus said unto him: 'Go thy way; thy faith hath made thee whole.' And immediately he received his sight, and followed Jesus in the way.

This man, Bartimaeus, was not a young man apparently; he had sat for a number of years at the gate of Jericho, receiving his sustenance from the mercy or the indifferent wealth of those who passed by. It is likely that in the course of his life he had tried all existing means and all possible ways of being healed. As a child, he had probably been brought to the temple, prayers and sacrifices had been offered. He had visited all those who could heal, either because they had a gift, or because they had knowledge. He had surely fought for his sight and he had been constantly disappointed. Every human device had been tried, yet blind he remained. He had probably also heard in the previous months that a young preacher had appeared in Galilee, a man who loved people, who was merciful and who was a holy man of God, a man who could heal and work miracles. He had probably often thought that if he could he would have gone to meet him; but Christ was going from one place to another and there was little chance that a blind man should find his way to him. And so, with that spark of hope that made despair even deeper and more acute, he sat by the gate of Jericho.

One day a crowd passed him, a crowd greater than usual, a noisy oriental crowd; the blind man heard it and asked who was there, and when he was told that it was Jesus of Nazareth, he began to call out. Every spark of hope that had survived in his soul suddenly became a fire, a burning fire of hope. Jesus, whom he had never been able to meet, was passing his way. He was passing by, and every step was bringing him nearer and nearer, and then every step would take him farther and farther away, hopelessly so; and he began to cry, 'Jesus, thou son of David, have mercy upon me.' This was the most perfect profession of faith that he could make at that moment. He recognised in him the son of David, the Messiah; he could not yet call him the son of God, because even the disciples did not yet know; but he recognised in him the one who was expected. Then something happened which happens constantly in our lives: they told him to be quiet.

How often does it not happen that after seeking and struggling for years on our own, when on a sudden we begin to cry to God, many voices try to silence our prayers, outward voices as well as inward voices. Is it worth praying? How many years did you struggle and God did not care? Is he to care now? What is the use of praying? Go back into your hopelessness, you are blind, and blind for ever. But the greater the opposition, the greater also is the evidence that help is at hand. The devil never attacks us so violently as when we are quite close to the term of our struggle, and we might yet be saved, but often are not, because we give way at the last moment. Give in, says the devil, make haste, it is too much, it is more than you can stand, you can put an end to it at once, do not wait, you cannot endure it any more. And then we commit suicide, physically, morally, spiritually; we renounce the struggle and accept death, just a minute before help was at hand and we might have been saved.

We must never listen to these voices; the louder they shout, the stronger should be our purpose; we must be ready to cry out as long as necessary, as loud as Bartimaeus did. Jesus Christ was passing by, his last hope was passing by, but the people who were surrounding Christ were either indifferent or trying to silence him. His grief and suffering were out of place. They, who perhaps needed

Christ less, but surrounded him, wanted him to be busy with them. Why should that blind man in distress interrupt them? But Bartimaeus knew that there was no hope for him if this last one vanished. This depth of hopelessness was the well from which sprang a faith, a prayer full of such conviction and such insistence that it broke through all barriers – one of those prayers which beat at the gates of heaven as St John Climacus says. Because his despair was so profound he did not listen to the voices commanding him to be quiet, to hold his peace; and the more they tried to prevent him from reaching out to Christ, the louder he said: 'Thou, son of David, have mercy on me!' Christ stood still, asked for him to be brought forward and worked a miracle.

We can learn from Bartimaeus in our practical approach to prayer that when we turn to God wholeheartedly, God always hears us. Usually when we realise that we can no longer depend upon all that we are accustomed to find reliable around us, we are not yet ready to renounce these things. We can see that there is no hope as far as human, earthly ways are concerned. We are aiming at something, we search for our sight and we are constantly frustrated; it is torment and hopelessness and if we stop there, we are defeated. But if at that moment we turn to God, knowing that only God is left, and say: 'I trust thee and commit into thy hands my soul and body, my whole life,' then despair has led us to faith.

Despair is conducive to a new spiritual life when we have got the courage to go deeper and farther, realising that what we are despairing about is not the final victory but the means we have employed to reach it. Then we

D

start at rock bottom in quite a new way. God may bring us back to one of the means we have already tried, but which, under him, we may be able to use successfully. There should always be real cooperation between God and man and then God will give intelligence, wisdom, power to do the right thing and achieve the right goal.

IV

Meditation and Worship

MEDITATION AND PRAYER are often confused, but there is no danger in this confusion if meditation develops into prayer; only when prayer degenerates into meditation. Meditation primarily means thinking, even when God is the object of our thoughts. If as a result we gradually go deeper into a sense of worship and adoration, if the presence of God grows so powerful that we become aware of being with God, and if gradually, out of meditation we move into prayer, it is right; but the contrary should never be allowed, and in this respect there is a sharp difference between meditation and prayer.

The main distinction between meditation and our usual haphazard thinking is coherence; it should be an ascetical exercise of intellectual sobriety. Theophane the Recluse, speaking of the way in which people usually think, says that thoughts buzz around in our heads like a swarm of mosquitoes, in all directions, monotonously, without order and without particular result.

The first thing to learn, whatever the chosen subject of thought, is to pursue a line. Whenever we begin to think of God, of things divine, of anything that is the life of the soul, subsidiary thoughts appear; on every side we see so many possibilities, so many things that are full of interest and richness; but we must, having chosen the subject of our thinking, renounce all, except the chosen one. This is the only way in which our thoughts can be kept straight and can go deep.

The purpose of meditation is not to achieve an academic exercise in thinking; it is not meant to be a purely intellectual performance, nor a beautiful piece of thinking without further consequences; it is meant to be a piece of straight thinking under God's guidance and Godwards, and should lead us to draw conclusions about how to live. It is important to realise from the outset that a meditation has been useful when, as a result, it enables us to live more precisely and more concretely in accordance with the gospel.

Every one of us is impervious to certain problems and open to others; when we are not yet accustomed to thinking, it is better to begin with something which is alive for us, either with those sayings which we find attractive, which 'make our heart burn within us', or else, on the contrary, with those against which we rebel, which we cannot accept; we find both in the gospel.

Whatever we take, a verse, a commandment, an event in the life of Christ, we must first of all assess its real objective content. This is extremely important because the purpose of meditation is not to build up a fantastic structure but to understand a truth. The truth is there, given, it is God's truth, and meditation is meant to be a bridge between our lack of understanding and the truth revealed.

It is a way in which we can educate our intelligence, and gradually learn to have 'the mind of Christ' as St Paul says (1 Cor 2:16).

To make sure of the meaning of the text is not always as simple as it sounds; there are passages that are quite easy, there are other passages where words are used which can be understood only against the background of our experience, or of the traditional understanding of these words. For instance, the phrase 'The Bride of the Lamb' can be understood only if we know what scripture means by the word 'Lamb'; otherwise it becomes completely nonsensical and will be misunderstood. There are words which we can understand adequately only if we ignore the particular or technical meaning they may have acquired.

One such word is 'spirit'. For a christian, 'spirit' is a technical work; it is either the Holy Spirit, the third person of the Trinity or one of the components of the human body – body and soul. It does not always convey with the same simplicity and breadth what the writers of the gospel meant to convey; it has become so specialised that it has lost contact with its root. To make sure of the text and what it means, there is also the definition given in the dictionary. The word spirit, or any other word, can be looked up and immediately seems simple and concrete, although it may have developed into a deeper meaning as a result of the efforts of theologians. But we should never start with the deeper meaning before we have got the simple concrete one, which everyone could understand at the time Christ spoke with the people around him.

There are things which we cannot understand except within the teaching of the Church; scripture must be understood with the mind of the Church, the mind of Christ, because the Church has not changed; in its inner experience it continues to live the same life as it lived in the first century; and words spoken by Paul, Peter, Basil or others within the Church, have kept their meaning. So, after a preliminary understanding in our own contemporary language, we must turn to what the Church means by the words; only then can we ascertain the meaning of the given text and have a right to start thinking and to draw conclusions. Once we have got the meaning of the text, we must see whether in its utter simplicity it does not already offer us suggestions, or even better, a straight command. As the aim of meditation, of understanding scripture, is to fulfil the will of God, we must draw practical conclusions and act upon them. When we have discovered the meaning, when in this sentence God has spoken to us, we must look into the matter and see what we can do, as in fact we do whenever we stumble on a good idea; when we come to realise that this or that is right, we immediately think how to integrate it into our life, in what way, on what occasion, by what method. It is not enough to understand what can be done and enthusiastically to start telling our friends all about it; we should start doing it. Paul the Simple, an Egyptian saint, once heard Anthony the Great read the first verse of the first Psalm: 'Blessed is the man that walketh not in the counsel of the ungodly,' and immediately, Paul departed into the wilderness. Only after some thirty years, when Anthony met him again, St Paul said to him with great humility: 'I have spent all this time trying to become the man that does not walk in the counsel of the ungodly.' We do not need understanding on many points to reach perfection; what we need is thirty years of work to try to understand and to become that new man.

Often we consider one or two points and jump to the next, which is wrong since we have just seen that it takes a long time to become recollected, what the Fathers call an attentive person, someone capable of paying attention to an idea so long and so well that nothing of it is lost. The spiritual writers of the past and of the present day will all tell us: take a text, ponder on it hour after hour, day after day, until you have exhausted all your possibilities, intellectual and emotional, and thanks to attentive reading and re-reading of this text, you have come to a new attitude. Quite often meditation consists in nothing but examining the text, turning over these words of God addressed to us, so as to become completely familiar with them, so imbued with them that gradually we and these words become completely one. In this process, even if we think that we have not found any particular intellectual richness, we have changed.

On many occasions we can do a lot of thinking; there are plenty of situations in our daily life in which we have nothing to do except wait, and if we are disciplined – and this is part of our spiritual training – we will be able to concentrate quickly and fix our attention at once on the subject of our thoughts, of our meditation. We must learn to do it by compelling our thoughts to attach themselves to one focus and to drop everything else. In the beginning, extraneous thoughts will intrude, but if we push them away constantly, time after time, in the end they will leave us in peace. It is only when by training, by exercise, by habit, we have become able to concentrate profoundly and quickly, that we can continue through life in a state of collectedness, in spite of what we are doing. However, to become aware of having extraneous thoughts, we must already have achieved some sort of collectedness. We can be in a crowd, surrounded by people and yet completely alone and untouched by what is going on; it depends on us whether to allow what is happening outside to become an event in our inner life or not; if we allow it to, our attention will break down, but if we do not, we can be completely isolated and collected in God's presence whatever happens around us. There is a story by Al Absihi about this sort of concentration. A Moslem's family used to keep a respectful silence whenever he had a visitor, but they knew that they could make as much noise as they wanted while he was praying, because at such times he heard nothing; in fact, one day he was not even disturbed by a fire that broke out in his house.

We may sometimes find ourselves in a group of people arguing hotly with no hope of a solution. We cannot leave without causing further disorder, but what we can do is mentally to withdraw, turn to Christ and say, 'I know that you are here, help!' And just be with Christ. If it did not sound so absurd one would say, make Christ present in the situation. Objectively he is always present, but there is some difference between being there objectively and being introduced by an act of faith into a given situation. One can do nothing but sit back and just remain with Christ and let the others talk. His presence will do more than anything one could say. And from time to time, in an unexpected way, if one keeps quiet and silent together with Christ, one will discover that one can say something quite sensible that would have been impossible in the heat of argument.

Parallel with mental discipline, we must learn to acquire a peaceful body. Whatever our psychological activity, our body reacts to it; and our bodily state determines to a certain degree the type or quality of our psychological activity. Theophane the Recluse, in his advice to anyone wishing to attempt the spiritual life, says that one of the conditions indispensable to success is never to permit bodily slackness: 'Be like a violin string, tuned to a precise note, without slackness or supertension, the body erect, shoulders back, carriage of the head easy, the tension of all muscles oriented towards the heart.' A great deal has been written and said about the ways in which one can make use of the body to increase one's ability to be attentive, but on a level accessible to many, Theophane's advice seems to be simple, precise and practical. We must learn to relax and be alert at the same time. We must master our body so that it should not intrude but make collectedness easier for us.

Meditation is an activity of thought, while prayer is the rejection of every thought. According to the teaching of the eastern Fathers, even pious thoughts and the deepest and loftiest theological considerations, if they occur during prayer, must be considered as a temptation and suppressed; because, as the Fathers say, it is foolish to think about God and forget that you are in his presence. All the spiritual guides of Orthodoxy warn us against replacing this meeting with God by thinking about him. Prayer is essentially standing face to face with God, consciously striving to remain collected and absolutely still and attentive in his presence, which means standing with an undivided mind, an undivided heart and an undivided will in the presence of the Lord; and that is not easy. Whatever our training may give us, there is always a short cut open at any time: undividedness can be attained by the person for whom the love of God is everything, who has broken all ties, who is completely given to God; then there is no longer personal striving, but the working of the radiant grace of God.

God must always be the focus of our attention for there are many ways in which this collectedness may be falsified; when we pray from a deep concern, we have a sense that our whole being has become one prayer and we imagine that we have been in a state of deep, real prayerful collectedness, but this is not true, because the focus of attention was not God; it was the object of our prayer. When we are emotionally involved, no alien thought intrudes, because we are completely concerned with what we are praying about; it is only when we turn to pray for some other person or need that our attention is suddenly dispersed, which means that it was not the thought of God, not the sense of his presence that was the cause of this concentration, but our human concern. It does not mean that human concern is of no importance, but it means that the thought of a friend can do more than the thought of God, which is a serious point.

One of the reasons why we find it so difficult to be attentive is that the act of faith which we make in affirming: 'God is here,' carries too little weight for us. We are intellectually aware that God is here, but not aware of it physically in a way that would collect and focus all our energies, thoughts, emotions and will, making us nothing but attention. If we prepare for prayer by a process of imagination: 'The Lord Christ is here, that is what he looks like, this is what I know about him, this is what he means to me . . .', the richer the image, the less real the presence, because it is an idol that is built which obscures the real presence. We can derive some help from it for a sort of emotional concentration, but it is not God's presence, the real, objective presence of God.

The early Fathers and the whole Orthodox tradition teach us that we must concentrate, by an effort of will, on the words of the prayer we pronounce. We must pronounce the words attentively, matter-of-factly, without trying to create any sort of emotional state, and we must leave it to God to arouse whatever response we are capable of.

St John Climacus gives us a simple way of learning to concentrate. He says: choose a prayer, be it the Lord's Prayer or any other, take your stand before God, become aware of where you are and what you are doing, and pronounce the words of the prayer attentively. After a certain time you will discover that your thoughts have wandered; then restart the prayer on the words or the sentence which was the last you pronounced attentively. You may have to do that ten times, twenty times or fifty times; you may, in the time appointed for your prayer, be able to pronounce only three sentences, three petitions and go no farther; but in this struggle you will have been able to concentrate on the words, so that you bring to God, seriously, soberly, respectfully, words of prayer which you are conscious of, and not an offering that is not yours, because you were not aware of it.

John Climacus also advises us to read the prayer of our choice without haste, in a monotonous way, slowly enough to have time to pay attention to the words, but not so slowly as to make the exercise dull; and to do it without trying to experience anything emotionally, because what we aim at is a relationship with God. We should never try to squeeze out of the heart any sort of feeling when we come to God; a prayer is a statement, the rest depends on God.

In this way of training a given amount of time is set apart for prayer, and if prayer is attentive, it does not matter what this length of time is. If you were meant to read three pages in your rule of prayer and saw that after half an hour you were still reading the first twelve words, of course it would raise a feeling of discouragement; therefore, the best way is to have a definite time and keep to it. You know the time fixed and you have the prayer material to make use of; if you struggle earnestly, quite soon you will discover that your attention becomes docile, because the attention is much more subject to the will than we imagine, and when one is absolutely sure that however one tries to escape, it must be twenty minutes and not a quarter of an hour, one just perseveres. St John Climacus trained dozens of monks by this simple device – a time limit, then merciless attention, and that is all.

The outward beauty of the liturgy must not seduce us into forgetting that sobriety in prayer is a very important feature in Orthodoxy. In the *Way of a Pilgrim* a village priest gives some very authoritative advice on prayer: 'If you want it to be pure, right and enjoyable, you must choose some short prayer, consisting of few but forcible words, and repeat it frequently, over a long period. Then you will find delight in prayer.' The same idea is to be found in the *Letters of Brother Lawrence*: 'I do not advise you to use multiplicity of words in prayer; many words and long discourses being often the occasions of wandering.'

John of Kronstadt was asked once how it was that priests, in spite of their training, experience wandering, intrusive thoughts, even in the course of the liturgy. The answer was: 'Because of our lack of faith.' We have not faith enough, faith being understood in the terms of St Paul as 'the evidence of things not seen' (Heb 11:1). But it would be a mistake to think that those distracting thoughts all come from outside; we must face the fact that they come from our own depths: they are our continual inner preoccupations coming to the fore, they are just the thoughts that usually fill our life, and the only way to get radically rid of unworthy thoughts is to change our outlook on life fundamentally. Again, as Brother Lawrence puts it in his eighth letter: 'One way to recollect the mind easily in the time of prayer, and preserve it more in tranquillity, is not to let it wander too far at other times; you should keep it strictly in the presence of God; and being accustomed to think of him often, you will find it easy to keep your mind calm at the time of prayer, or at least to recall it from its wanderings.'

As long as we care deeply for all the trivialities of life, we cannot hope to pray wholeheartedly; they will always colour the train of our thoughts. The same is true about our daily relations with other people, which should not consist merely of gossip but be based on what is essential in every one of us, otherwise we may find ourselves unable to reach another level when we turn to God. We must eradicate everything meaningless and trivial in ourselves and in our relations with others, and concentrate on those things we shall be able to take with us into eternity.

It is not possible to become another person the moment we start to pray, but by keeping watch on one's thoughts one learns gradually to differentiate their value. It is in our daily life that we cultivate the thoughts which irrepressibly spring up at the time of prayer. Prayer in its turn will change and enrich our daily life, becoming the foundation of a new and real relationship with God and those around us.

In our struggle for prayer the emotions are almost irrelevant; what we must bring to God is a complete, firm determination to be faithful to him and strive that God should live in us. We must remember that the fruits of prayer are not this or that emotional state, but a deep change in the whole of our personality. What we aim at is to be made able to stand before God and to concentrate on his presence, all our needs being directed Godwards, and to be given power, strength, anything we need that the will of God may be fulfilled in us. That the will of God should be fulfilled in us is the only aim of prayer, and it is also the criterion of right prayer. It is not the mystical feeling we may have, or our emotions that make good praying. Theophane the Recluse says: 'You ask yourself, "Have I prayed well today?" Do not try to find out how deep your emotions were, or how much deeper you understand things divine; ask yourself: "Am I doing God's will better than I did before?" If you are, prayer has brought its fruits, if you are not, it has not, whatever amount of understanding or feeling you may have derived from the time spent in the presence of God.'

Concentration, whether in meditation or in prayer, can only be achieved by an effort of will. Our spiritual life is based on our faith and determination, and any incidental joys are a gift of God. St Seraphim of Sarov, when asked what it was that made some people remain sinners and never make any progress while others were becoming saints and living in God, answered: 'Only determination.' Our activities must be determined by an act of will, which usually happens to be contrary to what we long for; this will, based on our faith, always clashes with another will, our instinctive one. There are two wills in us, one is the conscious will, possessed to a greater or lesser degree, which consists in the ability to compel ourselves to act in accordance with our convictions. The second one is something else in us, it is the longings, the claims, the desires of all our nature, quite often contrary to the first will. St Paul speaks of two laws that fight against each other (Rom 7:23). He speaks of the old and the new Adam in us, who are at war. We know that one must die in order that the other should live, and we must realise that our spiritual life, our life as a human being taken as a whole, will never be complete as long as these two wills do not coincide. It is not enough to aim at the victory of the good will against the evil one; the evil one, that is the longings of our fallen nature, must absolutely, though gradually, be transformed into a longing, a craving for God. The struggle is hard and far-reaching.

The spiritual life, the christian life does not consist in developing a strong will capable of compelling us to do

what we do not want. In a sense, of course, it is an achievement to do the right things when we really wish to do the
wrong ones, but it remains a small achievement. A mature
spiritual life implies that our conscious will is in accordance
with the words of God and has remoulded, transformed our
nature so deeply, with the help of God's grace, that the
totality of our human person is only one will. To begin
with, we must submit and curb our will into obedience to
the commandments of Christ, taken objectively, applied
strictly, even when they clash with what we know about
life. We must, in an act of faith, admit against the evidence
that Christ is right. Experience teaches us that certain
things do not seem to work as the gospels say they should;
but God says they do, so they must. We must also remember that when we fulfil God's will in this objective
sense, we must not do it tentatively, thinking of putting it
to the test, to see what comes of it, because then it does not
work. Experience teaches us that when we are slapped on
one cheek, we want to retaliate; Christ says 'turn the other
cheek'. What we really expect when we finally determine
to turn the other cheek is to convert the enemy and win
his admiration. But when instead we are slapped again, we
are usually surprised or indignant, as though God has
cheated us into doing something quite unworkable.

We must outgrow this attitude, be prepared to do
God's will and pay the cost. Unless we are prepared to pay
the cost, we are wasting our time. Then, as a next step,
we must learn that doing is not enough, because we must
not be drilled into christianity, but we must *become*
christians; we must learn, in the process of doing the will
of God, to understand God's purpose. Christ has made his

intentions clear to us and it is not in vain that in St John's gospel he no longer calls us servants but friends, because the servant does not know the mind of the master, and he has told us all things (Jn 15:15). We must, by doing the will of God, learn what this doing implies, so that in thought, in will, in attitude, we may become co-workers with Christ (1 Cor 3:9). Being of one mind we shall gradually become inwardly what we try to be outwardly.

We see that we cannot partake deeply of the life of God unless we change profoundly. It is therefore essential that we should go to God in order that he should transform and change us, and that is why, to begin with we should ask for conversion. Conversion in Latin means a turn, a change in the direction of things. The Greek word *metanoia* means a change of mind. Conversion means that instead of spending our lives looking in all directions, we should follow one direction only. It is a turning away from a great many things which we valued solely because they were pleasant or expedient for us. The first impact of conversion is to modify our sense of values: God being at the centre of all, everything acquires a new position and a new depth. All that is God's, all that belongs to him, is positive and real. Everything that is outside him has no value or meaning. But it is not a change of mind alone that we can call conversion. We can change our minds and go no farther; what must follow is an act of will and unless our will comes into motion and is redirected Godwards, there is no conversion; at most there is only an incipient, still dormant and inactive change in us. Obviously it is not enough to look in the right direction and never move. Repentance must not be mistaken for remorse, it does not consist in

E

feeling terribly sorry that things went wrong in the past; it is an active, positive attitude which consists in moving in the right direction. It is made very clear in the parable of the two sons (Mt 21:28) who were commanded by their father to go to work at his vineyard. The one said, 'I am going', but did not go. The other said, 'I am not going', and then felt ashamed and went to work. This was real repentance, and we should never lure ourselves into imagining that to lament one's past is an act of repentance. It is part of it of course, but repentance remains unreal and barren as long as it has not led us to doing the will of the father. We have a tendency to think that it should result in fine emotions and we are quite often satisfied with emotions instead of real, deep changes.

When we have hurt someone and realise that we were wrong, quite often we go and express our sorrow to the person, and when the conversation has been emotionally tense, when there were a lot of tears and forgiveness and moving words, we go away with a sense of having done everything possible. We have wept together, we are at peace and now everything is all right. It is not all right at all. We have simply delighted in our virtues and the other person, who may be goodhearted and easily moved, has reacted to our emotional scene. But this is just what conversion is not. No one asks us to shed tears, nor to have a touching encounter with the victim, even when the victim is God. What is expected is that having understood the wrong, we should put it right.

Nor does conversion end there; it must lead us farther in the process of making us different. Conversion begins but it never ends. It is an increasing process in which we gradually become more and more what we should be, until, after the day of judgement, these categories of fall, conversion and righteousness disappear and are replaced by new categories of a new life. As Christ says: 'I make all things new' (Rev 21:5).

One can pray everywhere and anywhere, yet there are places where prayer finds its natural climate; those places are churches, fulfilling the promise; 'I will make them joyful in my house of prayer' (Is 56:7).

A church, once consecrated, once set part, becomes the dwelling-place of God. He is present there in another way than in the rest of the world. In the world he is present as a stranger, as a pilgrim, as one who goes from door to door, who has nowhere to rest his head; he goes as the lord of the world who has been rejected by the world and expelled from his kingdom and who has returned to it to save his people. In church he is at home, it is his place; he is not only the creator and the lord by right but he is recognised as such. Outside it he acts when he can and how he can; inside a church he has all power and all might and it is for us to come to him.

When we build a church or set apart a place of worship we do something which reaches far beyond the obvious significance of the fact. The whole world which God created has become a place where men have sinned; the devil has been at work, a fight is going on constantly; there is no place on this earth which has not been soiled by blood, suffering or sin. When we choose a minute part of it, calling upon the power of God himself, in rites which convey his grace, to bless it, when we cleanse it from the presence of the evil spirit and set it apart to be God's foothold on earth, we reconquer for God a small part of this desecrated world. We may say that this is a place where the kingdom of God reveals itself and manifests itself with power. When we come to church we should be aware that we are entering upon sacred ground, a place which belongs to God, and we should behave accordingly.

The icons seen on church walls are not merely images or paintings: an icon is a focus of real presence. St John Chrysostom advises us, before we start praying, to take our stand in front of an icon and to shut our eyes. He says 'shut your eyes', because it is not by examining the icon, by using it as a visual aid, that we are helped by it to pray. It is not a substantial presence in the sense in which the bread and wine are the body and blood of Christ. An icon is not, in this sense, Christ, but there is a mysterious link between the two. By the power of grace an icon participates in something which can best be defined in the words of Gregory Palamas as the energies of Christ, as the active power of Christ working for our salvation.

An icon is painted as an act of worship. The wood is chosen and blessed, the paint is blessed, the man who wishes to paint prepares himself by fasting, by confession, by communion. He keeps ascetical rules while working and when his work is completed, it is blessed with holy water and chrismated (this last part of the blessing is now often omitted, unfortunately). Thus, by the power of the Holy Spirit, the icon becomes more than a painting. It is loaded with presence, imbued with the grace of the Spirit and linked with the particular saint it represents in and through the mystery of the communion of saints and the cosmic unity of all things. One cannot say of the icon that the indwelling of the saint is identical with or even similar to that which we find in the holy gifts, and yet it is a focus of real presence as it is experienced and taught by the Church. An icon is not a likeness, it is a sign. Certain icons have been singled out by the power and wisdom of God to be miraculous icons. When you stand in their presence you feel challenged by them.

A priest who visited Russia recently took services in a church where there was a well-known wonder-working icon of Our Lady and was deeply conscious of her active participation in the service. The icon had become very dark in the course of centuries, and from the place where he stood he could not distinguish the features, so he continued to celebrate with his eyes shut. Suddenly he felt that the Mother of God in the icon was as it were compelling him to pray, directing his prayers, shaping his mind. He became aware of a power originating from the icon that filled the church with prayer and guided the diffuse thoughts. It was almost a physical presence, there was a person standing there, compelling a response.

V

Unanswered Prayer and Petition

IN THE EPISODE of the Canaanite woman (Mt 15: 22) we see Christ, at least at first, refusing to answer a prayer; it is the case of a prayer tested in an extremely hard way. The woman asks for something which is absolutely right, she comes with complete faith and does not even say 'if you can', she just comes, sure that Christ can and that he will be willing, and that her child will be cured. To all this faith the answer is 'No'. It is not that the prayer is not worthy, or the faith not sufficient, simply that she is the wrong sort of person. Christ has come for the Jews, she is a pagan; he has not come for her. But she insists, saying, 'Yes, I am the wrong kind, but even the dogs eat the crumbs which fall from their master's table.' And she stands, trusting in the love of God, in spite of what God says, trusting so humbly despite the reason he gives. She does not even invoke the love of God, she just appeals to its expression in daily life: I have no right to a loaf, just give me some crumbs. Christ's clear and sharp refusal tests her faith and her prayer is fulfilled.

So often we implore God, saying, 'O God, if . . . if

Thou wilt . . . if Thou canst . . .', just like the father, who says to Christ: 'Your disciples have not been able to cure my little boy, if you can do anything, do it' (Mk 9:22). Christ answers with another 'if': if you believe, however little, everything is possible with faith. Then the man says: 'I believe, help thou mine unbelief.' The two 'ifs' are correlative, because if there is no faith there is also no possibility for God to enter into the situation.

The fact that one turns to God should be the proof of belief, but it is so only to a certain extent; we believe and we do not believe at the same time, and faith shows its measure by overcoming its own doubts. When we say: 'Yes, I doubt, but I do believe in God's love more than I trust my own doubts,' it becomes possible for God to act. But if one believes in law and not in grace, if one believes that the world as we know it with its mechanical laws is mechanical because God willed it to be nothing but a machine, then there is no place for God. Yet the heart's experience, as well as modern science, teaches us that there is no such thing as the absolute law in which men believed in the nineteenth century. Whenever by faith the kingdom of God is re-created, there is a place for the laws of the kingdom to act, that is for God to come into the situation with his wisdom, his ability to do good within an evil situation, without, however, upsetting the whole world. Our 'if' refers less to the power of God than to his love and concern; and God's reply 'if you can believe in my love, everything is possible' means that no miracle can happen unless, even in an incipient way, the kingdom of God is present.

A miracle is not the breaking of the laws of the fallen

world, it is the re-establishment of the laws of the kingdom of God; a miracle happens only if we believe that the law depends not on the power but on the love of God. Although we know that God is almighty, as long as we think that he does not care, no miracle is possible; to work it God would have to enforce his will, and that he does not do, because at the very core of his relationship to the world, even fallen, there is his absolute respect for human freedom and rights. The moment you say: 'I believe, and that is why I turned to you,' implies: 'I believe that you will be willing, that there is love in you, that you are actually concerned about every single situation.' The moment this grain of faith is there the right relationship is established and a miracle becomes possible.

Apart from this type of 'if', which refers to our doubt in the love of God, and which is wrong, there is a legitimate category of 'if'. We can say: 'I am asking this, if it is according to thy will, or if it is for the best, or if there is no secret evil intention in me when I ask,' and so on. All these 'ifs' are more than legitimate, because they imply a diffident attitude to our own selves; and every prayer of petition should be an 'if-prayer'.

As the Church is an extension of Christ's presence in time and space, any christian prayer should be Christ praying although it implies a purity of heart that we do not possess. The prayers of the Church are Christ's prayers, particularly in the canon of the liturgy, where it is entirely Christ praying; but any other prayer in which we ask for something involving a concrete situation is always under 'if'. In the majority of cases we do not know what Christ would have prayed for in this situation and so we introduce

the 'if', which means that as far as we can see, as far as we
know God's will, this is what we wish to happen to meet
his will. But the 'if' also means: I am putting into these
words my desire that the best should happen, and therefore
you can alter this concrete petition to anything you choose,
taking my intention, the desire that your will be done,
even if I am unwise in stating how I should like it to be
done (Rom 8:26). When, for example, we pray for someone to recover, or to be back from a journey at a certain
time, for some purpose we think essential, our real intention is the good of the person, but we are not clear-
sighted about it, and our timing and planning may be
wrong. 'If' implies that so far as I can see what is right, be
it done that way, but if I am mistaken, do not take me at
my word but at my intention. The Staretz Ambrose of
Optina had the kind of vision which allowed him to see a
person's real good. The monastery's icon painter had just
received a large sum of money and was about to start his
journey home. He must have prayed that he might be on
his way immediately; but the Staretz deliberately delayed
the artist for three days, and in so doing saved him from
being murdered and robbed by one of his workmen. When
he eventually departed the villain had left his ambush, and
it was only years later that the painter discovered from what
danger the Staretz had protected him.

We sometimes pray for someone we love, who is in
need and whom we are not able to help. Very often we do
not know what the right thing is, we do not find the words
to help even the most beloved. Sometimes we know that
nothing can be done except to be silent, though we are
ready to give our life to help. In that spirit we can turn to

God, put the whole situation into his care and say: 'O God, who knowest everything and whose love is perfect, take this life into thine hand, do what I long to do, but cannot.' Prayer being a commitment, we cannot pray in all truth for those whom we are not ourselves prepared to help. With Isaiah we must be ready to hear the Lord say 'Whom shall I send, and who will go for us?' and to answer: 'Here am I, send me' (Is 6:8).

Many are dismayed at the thought of praying for the dead, and they wonder what one is aiming at, what one can hope in doing so. Can the destiny of the dead be changed if one prays for them, will the praying convince God to do an injustice and grant them what they have not deserved?

If you believe that prayers for the living are a help to them, why should you not pray for the dead? Life is one, for as St Luke says: 'He is not the God of the dead but of the living' (20:38). Death is not an end but a stage in the destiny of man, and this destiny is not petrified at the moment of death. The love which our prayer expresses cannot be in vain; if love had power on earth and had no power after death it would tragically contradict the word of scripture that love is as strong as death (Song 8:6), and the experience of the Church that love is more powerful than death, because Christ has defeated death in his love for mankind. It is an error to think that man's connection with life on earth ends with his death. In the course of one's life one sows seeds. These seeds develop in the souls of other men and affect their destiny, and the fruit that is born of these seeds truly belongs not only to those who bear it but also to those who sow. The words written or spoken that change a human life or the destiny of mankind, as the words of preachers, philosophers, poets or politicians, remain their authors' responsibility, not only for evil but also for good; the authors' destiny is bound to be affected by the way they have influenced those living after them.

The life of every person continues to have repercussions until the last judgement, and man's eternal and final destiny is determined not only by the short space of time he has lived on this earth but also by the results of his life, by its good or evil consequences. Those who have received seed sown as in fertile ground, can influence the destiny of the departed by prayerfully beseeching God to bless the man who has transformed their lives, given a meaning to their existence. In turning to God in an act of enduring love, faithfulness and gratitude they enter this eternal kingdom which transcends the limits of time, and they can influence the destiny and the situation of the departed. It is not injustice that is asked of God; we do not ask him merely to forgive a man in spite of what he has done but to bless him because of the good he has done, to which other lives bear witness.

Our prayer is an act of gratitude and love, in so far as our life is the continuation of something that he stood for. We do not ask God to be unjust, and we do not imagine that we are more compassionate and more loving than he is, nor do we ask him to be more merciful than he would otherwise be; we are bringing new evidence for God's judgement, and we pray that this evidence should be taken into account and that the blessing of God should come abundantly for the one who has meant so much in our life. It is important to realise that we pray not in order to convince God of something but to bear witness that this person has not lived in vain, neither loving nor inspiring love.

Any person who has been the origin of love in any way has something to put forward in his defence, but it is for those who remain to bear witness to what he has done for them. Here again it is not simply a matter of goodwill or emotion. St Isaac of Syria says: do not reduce your prayer to words, make the totality of your life a prayer to God. Therefore, if we wish to pray for our departed, our life must back up the prayer. It is not enough to wake up to a certain feeling for them from time to time and then ask God to do something for them. It is essential that every seed of good, truth and holiness that has been sown by them should bear fruit, because then we can stand before God and say: he has sown good, there was some quality in him which inspired me to do well, and this particle of good is not mine but his and is in a way his glory and his redemption.

The Orthodox Church has very firm views about death and burial. The burial service starts by 'Blessed is our God'; we should realise what weight this carries, because these words are said in spite of the death, in spite of the bereavement, in spite of the suffering. The service is based on Matins, which is a service of praise and light, the mourners stand holding lighted candles in their hands as a symbol of the resurrection. The basic idea of the service is that we are indeed faced with death, but death does not frighten us any more when we see it through the resurrection of Christ.

At the same time the service gives a sense of the ambiguity of death, the two sides to it. Death cannot be accepted, it is a monstrosity: we have been created in order to live, and yet in the world which human sin has made monstrous, death is the only way out. If our world of sin were fixed unchangeable and eternal, it would be hell; death is the only thing that allows the earth, together with suffering and sin, to escape from this hell.

The Church perceives the two sides to this; St John of Damascus has written about it with extreme realism, crudely, because a Christian cannot be romantic about death. Dying is dying in the same way in which, when we speak of the cross, we must remember that it is an instrument of death. Death is death with all its tragic ugliness and monstrosity, and yet death ultimately is the only thing that gives us hope. On the one hand, we long to live; on the other hand, if we long sufficiently to live, we long to die, because in this limited world it is impossible to live fully. There is decay indeed, but a decay which, in conjunction with the grace of God, leads to a measure of life which otherwise we would never have. 'Death is a gain,' says St Paul (Phil 1:21), because living in the body we get separated from Christ. When we have reached a certain measure of life – independent of time – we must shed this limited life to enter into unlimited life.

The Orthodox burial service is strikingly centred round the open coffin, because the person is still considered in his entirety as body and soul, both being the concern of the Church. The body has been prepared for the burial; the body is not a piece of outworn clothing, as some seemingly devout people like to say, which has been cast off for the soul to be free. A body is much more than this for a Christian; there is nothing that befalls the soul in which the body does not take part. We receive impressions of this world, but also of the divine world partly through the body. Every sacrament is a gift of God, conferred on the soul by means of physical actions; the waters of baptism, the oil of chrismation, the bread and wine of communion are all taken from the material world. We can never do either good or evil otherwise than in conjunction with our body. The body is not there only, as it were, for the soul to be born, mature and then to go, abandoning it; the body, from the very first day to the last, has been the co-worker of the soul in all things and is, together with the soul, the total man. It remains marked for ever as it were by the imprint of the soul and the common life they had together. Linked with the soul, the body is also linked through the sacraments to Jesus Christ himself. We commune to his blood and body, and the body is thus united in its own right with the divine world with which it comes into contact.

A body without a soul is a corpse and not our concern, and a soul without a body, even the soul of a saint that goes 'straight to heaven', does not yet enjoy the bliss which the whole human being is called to enjoy at the end of time when the glory of God shines through soul and body.

As St Isaac the Syrian says, even eternal bliss cannot be enforced on the human being without the consent of the body. It is extremely striking to find this comment upon the importance of the body in the sayings of St Isaac, who is one of the great ascetics, one of those about whom people might easily say that he spent all his life killing his body. But in the words of St Paul, the ascetics were killing the body of sin, to reap out of corruption, eternity (Rom 6:6) and not killing the body for the soul to escape an imprisonment.

Thus the dead body is an object of care on the part of the Church, even when it is the body of a sinner; and all the attention we pay to it when alive is nothing to the veneration shown it at the burial service.

In the same way the body is linked with the soul in the life of prayer. Every perversity, every excess, every vulgarity to which we ourselves subject our bodies degrades one member of this partnership in a way which damages the other; to put the matter another way, indignity imposed from without can be overcome by prayer; self-inflicted indignity destroys prayer.

The characteristic of christian prayer is that it is the prayer of Christ, brought to his father, from generation to generation in constantly renewed situations, by those who, by grace and participation, are Christ's presence in this world; it is a continuous, unceasing prayer to God, that God's will should be done, that all should happen according to his wise and loving plan. This means that our life of prayer is at the same time a struggle against all that is not Christ's. We prepare the ground for our prayer each time we shed something which is not Christ's, which is unworthy of him, and only the prayer of one who can, like St Paul, say: 'I live, yet not I, but Christ liveth in me' (Gal 2:20) is real christian prayer.

Yet, instead of praying for the will of God to be done, we often try to convince him to do things as we want. How can such prayers not be defeated?

However well we pray, we must be aware at every moment that our best idea may be wrong. However sincere, however truthful our intentions, however perfect it is according to our lights, every prayer may go wrong at a certain moment, and this is why, when we have said everything we had to say to God, we must add, as Christ did in the garden of Gethsemane: 'Not as I will, but as Thou wilt' (Mt 26:39). In the same spirit we may make use of the intercession of the saints: we bring them our intentions which are good, but let them frame them in accordance with the will of God, which they know.

'Ask and it shall be given' (Mt 7:7). These words are a thorn in the christian consciousness, they can neither be accepted nor rejected. To reject them would mean a refusal of God's infinite kindness, but we are not yet christian enough to accept them. We know that the father would not give a stone instead of bread (Mt 7:9), but we do not think of ourselves as children who are unconscious of their real needs and what is good or bad for them. Yet there lies the explanation of so many unanswered prayers. It can also be found in the words of St John Chrysostom: 'Do not be distressed if you do not receive at once what you ask for: God wants to do you more good through your perseverance in prayer.'

'Could not the silence of God be the tragic aspect of our own deafness?'*

'Again I say unto you that if two of you shall agree on earth as touching anything that they shall ask, it shall be done for them of my Father which is in heaven' (Mt

* A. de Chateaubriant, *La Réponse du Seigneur*, p. 170.

18:19). This quotation is sometimes used as a stick with which to beat christians, because often enough things are asked earnestly by several persons together and yet not granted. But objections crumble the moment it appears that the being together is a wordly one, the agreement is coalition and not unity, and the belief that God can do anything he likes is interpreted in the same way that it was by Job's comforters.

As for the seeming untruth that 'All things, whatsoever Ye shall ask in prayer, believing, ye shall receive' (Mt 21:22), it is answered by Christ's prayer in the garden of Gethsemane and partly also by St Paul (Heb 11:36-40):

> And others had trial of cruel mockings and scourgings, yea moreover of bonds of imprisonment: They were stoned, they were sawn asunder, were tempted, were slain with the sword; they wandered about in sheepskins and goatskins; being destitute, afflicted, tormented; (of whom the world was not worthy) they wandered in deserts, and in mountains, and in dens and caves of the earth. And all these, having obtained a good report through faith, received not the promise. God having provided some better things for us, that they, without us, should not be made perfect.

Surely in all those situations there was a great deal of prayer, not perhaps for deliverance on the part of those who were ready to lay down their lives for God, but for help; and yet they were not given all they could expect.

When God sees that you have faith enough to stand his silence or to accept being delivered to torment, moral or physical, for a greater fulfilment of his kingdom, he may keep silent, and in the end the prayer will be answered, but in quite a different way from what you expected.

F

St Paul says, speaking of the prayer of Christ in the garden of Gethsemane, that his prayer was heard (Heb 5:7), and God raised him from the dead. St Paul does not speak here of an immediate answer from God, who could have taken away the cup, which was what Christ was asking; but in fact God gave Christ strength to accept, to suffer, to fulfil his work, and it is the absoluteness of his faith which made it possible for God to say No. But it is also this very absoluteness of Christ's faith which made it possible for the world to be saved.

Many of our prayers are prayers of petition, and people seem to think that petition is the lowest level of prayer; then comes gratitude, then praise. But in fact it is gratitude and praise that are expressions of a lower relationship. On our level of half-belief it is easier to sing hymns of praise or to thank God than to trust him enough to ask something with faith. Even people who believe half-heartedly can turn to thank God when something nice comes their way; and there are moments of elation when everyone can sing to God. But it is much more difficult to have such undivided faith as to ask with one's whole heart and whole mind with complete confidence. No one should look askance at petition, because the ability to say prayers of petition is a test of the reality of our faith.

When the Mother of Zebedee's children came to ask Christ for the two best places in paradise for her two sons, she came with complete confidence that the Lord could do what she was asking, but she was thinking of the power of Christ to grant her request as the Lord's right to act simply according to his will, which was not in accordance with the teaching: 'My judgement is just because I seek not mine own will, but the will of the Father which hath sent me' (Jn 5:30).

What the Mother of Zebedee's children expected was that the Lord would arbitrarily fulfil her desire as a favour, because she was the first to put forward the claim. The refusal of Christ pointed out that what the mother was asking was for a situation of pride in the kingdom of God, when the whole kingdom is based on humility. The mother's prayer was conditioned by the Old Testament attitude to the coming of the Messiah.

VI

The Jesus Prayer

THOSE WHO HAVE read *The Way of a Pilgrim* are familiar with the expression 'The Jesus Prayer'. It refers to a short prayer the words of which are: 'Lord Jesus Christ, Son of God, have mercy on me, a sinner,' constantly repeated. *The Way of a Pilgrim* is the story of a man who wanted to learn to pray constantly (I Thes 5:17). As the man whose experience is being related is a pilgrim, a great many of his psychological characteristics, and the way in which he learned and applied the prayer, were conditioned by the fact that he lived in a certain way, which makes the book less universally applicable than it could be; and yet it is the best possible introduction to this prayer, which is one of the greatest treasures of the Orthodox Church.

The prayer is profoundly rooted in the spirit of the gospel, and it is not in vain that the great teachers of Orthodoxy have always insisted on the fact that the Jesus Prayer sums up the whole of the gospel. This is why the Jesus Prayer can only be used in its fullest sense if the person who uses it belongs to the gospel, is a member of the Church of Christ.

All the messages of the gospel, and more than the messages, the reality of the gospel, is contained in the name, in the person of Jesus. If you take the first half of the prayer you will see how it expresses our faith in the Lord: 'Lord Jesus Christ, Son of God.' At the heart we find the name of Jesus; it is the name before whom every knee shall bow (Is 45:23), and when we pronounce it we affirm the historical event of the incarnation. We affirm that God, the Word of God, co-eternal with the father, became man, and that the fullness of the godhead dwelt in our midst (Col 2:9) bodily in his person.

To see in the man of Galilee, in the prophet of Israel, the incarnate Word of God, God become man, we must be guided by the spirit, because it is the spirit of God who reveals to us both the incarnation and the lordship of Christ. We call him Christ, and we affirm thereby that in him were fulfilled the prophecies of the Old Testament. To affirm that Jesus is the Christ implies that the whole history of the Old Testament is ours, that we accept it as the truth of God. We call him son of God, because we know that the Messiah expected by the Jews, the man who was called 'son of David' by Bartimaeus, is the incarnate son of God. These words sum up all we know, all we believe about Jesus Christ, from the Old Testament to the New, and from the experience of the Church through the ages. In these few words we make a complete and perfect profession of faith.

But it is not enough to make this profession of faith; it is not enough to believe. The devils also believe and tremble (Jas 2:19). Faith is not sufficient to work salvation, it must lead to the right relationship with God; and so, having professed, in its integrity, sharply and clearly, our faith in the lordship and in the person, in the historicity and in the divinity of Christ, we put ourselves face to face with him, in the right state of mind: 'Have mercy on me, a sinner.'

These words 'have mercy' are used in all the Christian Churches and, in Orthodoxy, they are the response of the people to all the petitions suggested by the priest. Our modern translation 'have mercy' is a limited and insufficient one. The Greek word which we find in the gospel and in the early liturgies is *eleison*. *Eleison* is of the same root as *elaion*, which means olive tree and the oil from it. If we look up the Old and New Testament in search of the passages connected with this basic idea, we will find it described in a variety of parables and events which allow us to form a complete idea of the meaning of the word. We find the image of the olive tree in Genesis. After the flood Noah sends birds, one after the other, to find out whether there is any dry land or not, and one of them, a dove – and it is significant that it is a dove – brings back a small twig of olive. This twig conveys to Noah and to all with him in the ark the news that the wrath of God has ceased, that God is now offering man a fresh opportunity. All those who are in the ark will be able to settle again on firm ground and make an attempt to live, and never more perhaps, if they can help it, undergo the wrath of God.

In the New Testament, in the parable of the good Samaritan, olive oil is poured to soothe and to heal. In the anointing of kings and priests in the Old Testament, it is again oil that is poured on the head as an image of the grace of God that comes down and flows on them (Ps 133:2) giving them new power to fulfil what is beyond human capabilities. The king is to stand on the threshold, between the will of men and the will of God, and he is called to lead his people to the fulfilment of God's will; the priest also stands on that threshold, to proclaim the will of God and to do even more: to act for God, to pronounce God's decrees and to apply God's decision.

The oil speaks first of all of the end of the wrath of God, of the peace which God offers to the people who have offended against him; further it speaks of God healing us in order that we should be able to live and become what we are called to be; and as he knows that we are not capable with our own strength of fulfilling either his will or the laws of our own created nature, he pours his grace abundantly on us (Rom 5:20). He gives us power to do what we could not otherwise do.

The words *milost* and *pomiluy* in slavonic have the same root as those which express tenderness, endearing, and when we use the words *eleison*, 'have mercy on us', *pomiluy*, we are not just asking God to save us from His wrath – we are asking for love.

If we turn back to the words of the Jesus Prayer, 'Lord Jesus Christ, Son of God, have mercy on me, a sinner', we see that the first words express with exactness and integrity the gospel faith in Christ, the historical incarnation of the Word of God; and the end of the prayer expresses all the complex rich relationships of love that exist between God and his creatures.

The Jesus Prayer is known to innumerable Orthodox, either as a rule of prayer or in addition to it, as a form of devotion, a short focal point that can be used at any moment, whatever the situation.

Numerous writers have mentioned the physical aspects

of the prayer, the breathing exercises, the attention which is paid to the beating of the heart and a number of other minor features. The Philocalia is full of detailed instructions about the prayer of the heart, even with references to the Sufi technique. Ancient and modern Fathers have dealt with the subject, always coming to the same conclusion: never to attempt the physical exercises without strict guidance by a spiritual father.

What is of general use, and God given, is the actual praying, the repetition of the words, without any physical endeavour – not even movements of the tongue – and which can be used systematically to achieve an inner transformation. More than any other prayer, the Jesus Prayer aims at bringing us to stand in God's presence with no other thought but the miracle of our standing there and God with us, because in the use of the Jesus Prayer there is nothing and no one except God and us.

The use of the prayer is dual, it is an act of worship as is every prayer, and on the ascetical level, it is a focus that allows us to keep our attention still in the presence of God.

It is a very companionable prayer, a friendly one, always at hand and very individual in spite of its monotonous repetitions. Whether in joy or in sorrow, it is, when it has become habitual, a quickening of the soul, a response to any call of God. The words of St Simeon, the new theologian, apply to all its possible effects on us: 'Do not worry about what will come next, you will discover it when it comes' (Quoted in the Guild of Pastoral Psychology, No. 95, p. 91).

VII

Ascetic Prayer

WHEN WE ARE in the right frame of mind, when the
heart is full of worship, of concern for others, when as St
Luke says, our lips speak from the fullness of the heart
(6:45), there is no problem about praying; we speak freely
to God in the words that are most familiar to us. But if we
were to leave our life of prayer at the mercy of our moods,
we should probably pray from time to time fervently and
sincerely, but lose for long periods any prayerful contact
with God. It is a great temptation to put off praying till the
moment when we feel alive to God, and to consider that
any prayer or any move Godwards at other periods lacks
sincerity. We all know from experience that we have a
variety of feelings which do not come to the fore at every
moment of our lives; illness or distress can blot them from
our consciousness. Even when we love deeply, there are
times when we are not aware of it and yet we know that
love is alive in us. The same is true with regard to God;
there are inner and outward causes that make it difficult
at times to be aware of the fact that we believe, that we have
hope, that we do love God. At such moments we must act

not on the strength of what we feel but of what we know. We must have faith in what is in us, although we do not perceive it at that particular moment. We must remember that love is still there, although it does not fill our hearts with joy or inspiration. And we must stand before God, remembering that he is always loving, always present, in spite of the fact that we do not feel it.

When we are cold and dry, when it seems that our prayer is a false pretence, carried out by routine, what should we do? Would it be better to stop praying until prayer comes alive again? But how shall we know that the time has come? There is a grave danger of being seduced by the desire for perfection in prayer when we are still so far from it. When prayer is dry, instead of giving way we should make a wider act of faith and carry on. We should say to God: 'I am worn out, I cannot pray really, accept, O Lord, this monotonous voice and the words of prayer, and help me.' Make prayer a matter of quantity when unable to make it a matter of quality. Of course, it is better to utter only 'Our Father', with all the depth of understanding of the words, than to repeat the Lord's Prayer twelve times; but it is just what we are sometimes incapable of. Prayer being quantitative does not mean the utterance of more words than usual; it means keeping to the usual rule of prayer fixed for oneself and accepting the fact that it is nothing but a certain quantity of repeated words. As the Fathers say, the Holy Spirit is always there when there is prayer and according to St Paul: 'No man can say that Jesus is the Lord, but by the Holy Ghost' (I Cor 12:3). It is the Holy Spirit who will in due time fill prayer, faithful and patient as it has been, with the meaning and depth of new life. When we stand before God in these moments of dejection we must use our will, we must pray from conviction if not from feeling, out of the faith we are aware of possessing, intellectually if not with a burning heart.

At such moments the prayers sound quite different to us, but not to God; as Julian of Norwich says, 'Pray inwardly though thou thinkest it savour thee not, for it is profitable, though thou feel not, though thou see nought, yea though thou think thou canst not. For in dryness and in barrenness, in sickness and in feebleness, then is thy prayer well pleasant to me, though thou thinkest it savour thee nought but little and so is all thy believing prayer in my sight' (*The Cloud of Unknowing*).

In those periods of dryness, when prayer becomes an effort, our main support is faithfulness and determination; it is by an act of will, including them both, that we compel ourselves, without considering our feelings, to take our stand before God and speak to him, simply because God is God and we are his creatures. Whatever we feel at a given moment our position remains the same; God remains our creator, our saviour, our lord and the one towards whom we move, who is the object of our longing and the only one who can give us fulfilment.

Sometimes we think that we are unworthy of praying and that we even have no right to pray; again, this is a temptation. Every drop of water, from wherever it comes, pool or ocean, is purified in the process of evaporation; and so is every prayer ascending to God. The more dejected we feel, the greater the necessity for prayer, and that is surely what John of Kronstadt felt one day when he was praying, watched by a devil who was muttering, 'You hypocrite, how dare you pray with your filthy mind, full of the thoughts I read in it.' He answered, 'It is just because my mind is full of thoughts I dislike and fight that I am praying to God.'

Whether it is the Jesus Prayer that is being used or any other readymade prayer, people often say: what right have I to use it? How can I say those words as my own? When we make use of prayers which have been written by saints, by men of prayer, and are the result of their experience, we can be sure that if we are attentive enough, the words will become our own, we shall grow into their underlying feeling and they will remould us by the grace of God, who responds to our effort. With the Jesus Prayer the situation, in a way, is simpler, because the worse our position is, the easier it is to realise that, having taken our stand before God, all we can say is *Kyrie Eleison*, 'Have mercy'.

More often than we may admit to ourselves, we pray hoping for a mysterious illumination, hoping that something will happen to us, that a thrilling experience will come our way. It is a mistake, the same kind of mistake we make sometimes in our relationships with people which may in fact destroy the relationship completely. We approach a person and we expect a definite sort of response, and when there is no response whatever or else when it is not the one we expected, we are disappointed, or we dismiss the reality of the given answer. When we pray, we must remember that the Lord God, who lets us come freely into his presence, is also free with regard to us; which does not mean that the freedom he takes is an arbitrary one, as ours, to be gracious or rude according to our mood, but that he is not bound to reveal himself to us simply because we have come and are gazing in his direction. It is very important to remember that both God and we are free either to come or to go; and this freedom is of immense importance because it is characteristic of a real relationship.

Once, a young woman, after a period of prayerful life in which God seemed to be immensely familiar and close, suddenly lost touch with him completely. But more than the sorrow of losing him she was afraid of the temptation of trying to escape that absence of God by building up a false presence of him; because the real absence of God and his real presence are equally good proofs of his reality and of the concreteness of the relationship which prayer implies.

So we must be prepared to offer our prayer and be ready for whatever God may give. This is the basic principle of the ascetic life. In the struggle to keep ourselves directed Godwards and to fight against anything in us that is opaque, that prevents us from looking in the direction of God, we can be neither altogether active nor passive. We cannot be active in the sense that, by agitating ourselves, by making efforts, we cannot climb into heaven or bring God down from heaven. But we cannot just be passive either and sit doing nothing, because God does not treat us as objects; there would be no true relationship if we were merely acted upon by him. The ascetic attitude is one of vigilance, the vigilance of a soldier who stands in the night as still as he can and as completely alert and aware as possible of anything that is happening around him, ready to respond in the right way and with speed to anything that may happen. In a way he is inactive because he stands and does nothing; on the other hand, it is intense activity, because he is alert and completely recollected. He listens, he watches with heightened perception, ready for anything.

In the inner life it is exactly the same. We must stand in God's presence in complete silence and collectedness, alert and unstirring. We may wait for hours, or for longer periods of time, but a moment will come when our alertness will be rewarded, because something will be happening. But again, if we are alert and vigilant, we are on the lookout for anything that may come our way, and not for one particular thing. We must be ready to receive from God whatever experience is sent. When we have prayed for some time and have felt a certain warmth, we fall quite easily into the temptation of coming to God the next day expecting the same thing to happen. If we have in the past prayed with warmth or with tears, with contrition or joy, we come to God looking forward to an experience we have already had, and quite often, because we are looking for the old one, we miss the new contact with God.

God's coming close to us may find expression in a variety of ways; it may be joy, it may be dread, it may be contrition or anything else. We must remember that what we are going to perceive today is something unknown to us, because God as we knew him yesterday is not God as he might reveal himself tomorrow.

VIII

The Prayer of Silence

PRAYER IS PRIMARILY an encounter with God: on certain occasions we may be aware of God's presence, more often dimly so, but there are times when we can place ourselves before him only by an act of faith, without being aware of his presence at all. It is not the degree of our awareness that is relevant, that makes this encounter possible and fruitful; other conditions must be fulfilled, the basic one being that the person praying should be real. In social life we have a variety of facets to our personalities. The same person appears as one in one setting and quite different in another, authoritative in any situation in which he commands, quite submissive at home, and again quite different among friends. Every self is complex, but none of these false personalities or of those which are partly false and partly true, are our real selves to such an extent as to be able to stand in our name in the presence of God. This weakens our prayer, it creates dividedness of mind, heart and will. As Polonius says in *Hamlet*: 'To thine own self be true, and it must follow as the night the day, Thou canst not then be false to any man.'

To find the real self, among and beyond those various false persons, cannot be done at an easy cost. We are so unaccustomed to be ourselves in any deep and true sense that we find it almost impossible to know where to begin the search. We all know that there are moments when we are nearer to being our true selves; those moments should be singled out and carefully analysed in order to make an approximate discovery of what we really are. It is our vanity that usually makes it so difficult to discover the truth about ourselves; our vanity in itself and in the way it determines our behaviour. Vanity consists of glorying in things that are devoid of value and of depending for our judgement about ourselves, and consequently for our whole attitude to life, on the opinion of people who should not have this weight for us; it is a state of dependence on other people's reactions to our personality.

Thus vanity is the first enemy to be attacked, although, as the Fathers say, it remains the last to be defeated. We find an instance of the defeat of vanity in the story of Zacchaeus (Lk 19:1), which can teach us a great deal. Zacchaeus was a rich man with social standing, he was an official of the Roman Empire, a publican who had a position to maintain. He was an important citizen of his little city; the attitude which is summed up in 'what will people say?' might have stopped him from meeting Christ. When Zacchaeus heard that Christ was passing through Jericho, his desire to see him was so strong that he forgot that he might become ridiculous – which is for us much worse than a great many evils – and he ran, this respectable citizen, and he climbed up a tree! He could be seen by the whole crowd and it is difficult to doubt that a great many laughed.

But such was his desire to meet Jesus that he forgot to worry about the opinions of other people; he became for a short time independent of anyone's judgement and at that moment he was completely himself; he was Zacchaeus the man, not Zacchaeus the publican, or the rich man, or the citizen.

Humiliation is one of the ways in which we may unlearn vanity, but unless it is accepted willingly, humiliation may only increase our hurt feelings and make us even more dependent on the opinions of others. Statements concerning vanity in St John Climacus and in St Isaac of Syria seem to conflict: one says that the only way to escape vanity is through pride; the other, that the way lies through humility. They both express their opinions in a given context and not as an absolute truth, but it allows us to see what the two extremes have in common, which is that whether you grow proud or humble, you take no notice of human opinions, in both cases the judgement of men is set aside. In the life of St Macarius we have an illustration of the first.

St Macarius, approaching a monastery over which he had oversight, saw several of the brethren laughing and mocking at a very young monk, who was taking no notice of them at all, and he was amazed at the serenity of the young man. Macarius had great experience of the difficulties of the spiritual struggle and thought it slightly suspicious. He asked the monk how it was that, young as he was, he had attained such a measure of impassibility. The answer was: 'Why should I take any notice of barking dogs? I pay no attention to them, God is the only one whom I accept as a judge.' This is an example of how pride

G

can free us from dependence upon the opinions of other people. Pride is an attitude in which we set ourselves at the centre of things, we become the criterion of truth, of reality, of good and evil, and then we are free from any other judgement and also free from vanity. But it is only perfect pride that can dispel vanity completely, and perfect pride is fortunately beyond our human capabilities.

The other remedy is humility. Basically humility is the attitude of one who stands constantly under the judgement of God. It is the attitude of one who is like the soil. Humility comes from the latin word *humus*, fertile ground. The fertile ground is there, unnoticed, taken for granted, always there to be trodden upon. It is silent, inconspicuous, dark and yet it is always ready to receive any seed, ready to give it substance and life. The more lowly, the more fruitful, because it becomes really fertile when it accepts all the refuse of the earth. It is so low that nothing can soil it, abase it, humiliate it; it has accepted the last place and cannot go any lower. In that position nothing can shatter the soul's serenity, its peace and joy.

There are moments when we are shaken out of our dependence on people's reactions; these are moments of profound sorrow and also of real overwhelming joy. When King David danced before the ark (II Sam 6:14), many, like Michal, the daughter of Saul, thought that the king was behaving in a very unseemly way. They probably smiled or turned away, embarrassed. But he was too full of joy to notice. It is the same with sorrow; when it is genuine and deep a person becomes real; poses and attitudes are forgotten and that is so precious in sorrow, in our own as much as in someone else's.

The difficulty is that when we are real because we are in sorrow, or because we are in joy, we are neither in a mood nor in a position to watch ourselves, to observe the features of our personality that come through; and yet there is a moment when we are still feeling deeply enough to be real, but sufficiently recovered from the ecstasy of joy or of grief as to be struck by the contrast between what we are at this particular moment and what we are usually; then our depth and our shallowness appear to us clearly. If we are attentive, if we do not move thoughtlessly from one state of mind and heart into the other, forgetting things as they pass by, we can gradually learn to preserve those characteristic features of reality which appear for a moment.

Several spiritual writers say that we must try to discover Christ in us. Christ is the perfect, completely true man and we can begin to discover what is true in us by discovering what is akin to him. There are passages in the gospel against which we rebel and other passages which make our heart burn within us (Lk 24:32). If we single out the passages which either provoke a revolt, or which we feel with all our heart to be true, we will already have discovered the two extremes in us; in short, the anti-Christ and the Christ in us. We must be aware of both kinds of passages and concentrate on those which are close to our heart, because we may safely assume that they mark one point at least in which Christ and we are akin, a point at which a man is already – certainly not fully, but at least in an incipient way – a real man, an image of Christ. But it is not enough to be emotionally moved, to give complete intellectual agreement to this or that passage of the gospel;

we must embody the words of Christ. We may have been touched and yet abandon all we have thought and felt on the first occasion that offers itself for applying the discovery.

There are times when we are in a mood to make peace with our enemies, but if the other person resists, the peace-making mood is soon changed into a bellicose one. That happened to Miusov, in Dostoyevsky's *The Brothers Kara-mazov*. He had just been rude and intolerant to others and then regained his own self-esteem by making a new start, but Karamazov's unexpected insolence at once changed his feelings again and 'Miusov passed immediately from the most benevolent frame of mind to the most savage. All the feelings that had subsided and died down in his heart revived instantly.'

It is not enough to be struck by the passages which appear to be so true, the struggle to become at every moment of our life what we are at the best moments must follow, and then we will gradually shed the superficial and become more real and more true; just as Christ is truth and reality itself, so shall we become more and more what Christ is. This does not consist in imitating Christ in his outer expression only, but of being inwardly what he is. The imitation of Christ is not an aping of his conduct or of his life; it is a hard and complex struggle.

This marks a difference between the Old and the New Testament: the commandments of the Old Testament were rules of life and he who faithfully kept to these rules became a righteous man, and yet he could not derive eternal life from them. On the contrary, the command-ments of the New Testament never make a man righteous. Christ once said to his disciples: 'When ye shall have done all those things which are commanded you, say, We are unprofitable servants; we have done that which was our duty to do' (Lk 17:10). But when we fulfil the commandments of Christ, not merely as rules of behaviour, but because the will of God has impregnated our heart, or even when we simply curb our ill-will into fulfilling them outwardly and stand in repentance, knowing that there is nothing in us beyond this outer compliance, we gradually grow into the knowledge of God, which is inward, not intellectual, rational or academic.

A person who has become real and true can stand before God and offer prayer with absolute attention, unity of intellect, heart and will, in a body that responds completely to the promptings of the soul. But until we have attained such perfection we can still stand in the presence of God, aware that we are partly real and partly unreal, and bring to him all that we can, but in repentance, confessing that we are still so unreal and so incapable of unity. At no moment of our life, whether we are still completely divided or in process of unification, are we deprived of the possibility of standing before God. But instead of standing in the complete unity that gives drive and power to our prayer, we can stand in our weakness, recognising it and ready to bear its consequences.

Ambrose of Optina, one of the last Russian Staretz, said once that two categories of men will attain salvation: those who sin and are strong enough to repent, and those who are too weak even to repent truly, but are prepared, patiently, humbly and gratefully, to bear all the weight of the consequences of their sins; in their humility they are acceptable to God.

God is always real, always himself, and if we could stand
face to face with him as he is and perceive his objective
reality, things might be simpler; but we manage, in a subjective way, to blur this truth, this reality in front of which
we stand, and to replace the real God by a pale picture of
him, even worse, by a God who is unreal because of our
one-sided and poor conception of him.

When we have to meet someone, the reality of the meeting does not depend only on what we are and on what the
other is, but very much on the preconceived idea we have
formed about the other person. It is not to the real person
we are then speaking, but to the image we have formed
and it usually takes a great deal of effort on the part of the
victim of this prejudice to break through and establish a
real relationship.

We have all formed ideas about God; however lofty,
beautiful, even true in its component parts the idea may be,
it will, if we are not careful, stand between us and the real
God and may become simply an idol before which we
pray while the real God is hidden by it. This happens
particularly when we turn to God with requests or for
intercession; then we do not come to God as to a person
with whom we want to share a difficulty, in whose love
we believe and from whom we expect a decision; but we
come trying to consider God under a certain aspect, and
we direct our prayers not towards God but towards a
concept of God, which at that particular moment is useful
to us.

We must not come to God in order to go through a
range of emotions, nor to have any mystical experience.
We must just come to God in order to be in his presence,

and, if he chooses to make us aware of it, blessed be God, but if he chooses to make us experience his real absence, blessed be God again, because as we have seen he is free to come near or not. He is as free as we are, although, when we do not come into God's presence, it is because we are busy with something else that attracts us more than he does. As for him, if he does not manifest his presence, it is because we must learn something about him and about ourselves. But the absence of God which we may perceive in our prayer, the sense that he is not there, is also part of the relationship and very valuable.

Our sense of God's absence may be the result of his will; he may want us to long for him and to learn how precious his presence is by making us know by experience what utter loneliness means. But often our experience of God's absence is determined by the fact that we do not give ourselves a chance of becoming aware of his presence. A woman who had been using the Jesus Prayer for fourteen years complained that she had never had any sense that God was there. But when she had it pointed out to her that she was talking all the time, she agreed to take her stand silently for a few days. As she was doing it she became aware that God was there, that the silence that surrounded her was not emptiness, absence of noise and agitation, but that there was a solidity in this silence, that it was not something negative, but positive, a presence, the presence of of God who made himself known to her by creating the same silence in her. And then she discovered that the prayer came up quite naturally again, but it was no longer the sort of discursive noise that had prevented God from making himself known.

If we were humble or even reasonable we should not expect, just because we had decided to pray, that we should at once have the experience of St John of the Cross, or St Theresa or St Seraphim of Sarov. However, it is not always the experience of the saints which we long to have, but simply to repeat a former one of our own; although to concentrate on a previous experience may blind us to the one which should come our way quite normally. Whatever we have felt belongs to the past and is linked with what we were yesterday, not with what we are today. We do not pray in order to provoke any particular experience in which we may delight, but in order to meet God with whatever may happen as a consequence, or to bring him what we have to bring and leave it to him to use it the way he chooses.

We must also remember that we should always approach God knowing that we do not know him. We must approach the unsearchable, mysterious God who reveals himself as he chooses; whenever we come to him, we are before a God we do not yet know. We must be open to any manifestation of his person and of his presence.

We may have understood a great deal about God from our own experience, from the experience of others, from the writings of the saints, from the teaching of the Church, from the witness of the scriptures; we may know that he is good, that he is humble, that he is a burning fire, that he is our judge, that he is our saviour and a great many other things, but we must remember that he may at any time reveal himself in a way in which we have never perceived him, even within these general categories. We must take our stand before him with reverence and be ready to meet whoever we shall meet, either the God who is already familiar or a God we cannot recognise. He may give us a sense of what he is and it may be quite different from what we expect. We hope to meet Jesus, mild, compassionate, loving, and we meet God who judges and condemns and will not let us come near in our present state. Or we come in repentance, expecting to be rejected, and we meet compassion. God, at every stage, is for us partly known and partly unknown. He reveals himself, and thus far we know him, but we shall never know him completely, there will always be the divine mystery, a core of mystery which we shall never be able to penetrate.

The knowledge of God can only be received and given in communion with God, only by sharing with God what he is, to the extent to which he is communicable. The Buddhist world of thought has illustrated it in a story about a doll of salt.

A doll of salt, after a long pilgrimage on dry land, came to the sea and discovered something she had never seen and could not possibly understand. She stood on the firm ground, a solid little doll of salt, and saw there was another ground that was mobile, insecure, noisy, strange and unknown. She asked the sea, 'But what are you?' and it said, 'I am the sea.' And the doll said, 'What is the sea?' to which the answer was, 'It is me.' Then the doll said, 'I cannot understand, but I want to; how can I?' The sea answered, 'Touch me.' So the doll shyly put forward a foot and touched the water and she got a strange impression that it was something that began to be knowable. She withdrew her leg, looked and saw that her toes had gone, and she was afraid and said, 'Oh, but where is my toe, what have you done to me?' And the sea said, 'You have given something in order to understand.' Gradually the water took away small bits of the doll's salt and the doll went farther and farther into the sea and at every moment she had a sense of understanding more and more, and yet of not being able to say what the sea was. As she went deeper, she melted more and more, repeating: 'But what is the sea?' At last a wave dissolved the rest of her and the doll said: 'It is I!' She had discovered what the sea was, but not yet what the water was.

Without drawing an absolute parallel between the buddhist doll and christian knowledge of God, one can see much truth in this little story. St Maxim uses the example of a sword that becomes red hot: the sword does not know where the fire ends and the fire does not know where the sword begins, so that one can, as he says, cut with fire and burn with iron. The doll knew what the sea was when she had become, minute as she was, the vastness of the sea. So also when we enter into the knowledge of God, we do not contain God, but are contained in him, and we become ourselves in this encounter with God, secure in his vastness.

Saint Athanasius said that man's ascent to deification begins from the moment he is created. From the first, God gives us uncreated grace to achieve union with him. From the Orthodox point of view there is no 'natural man' to whom grace is super-added. The first word of God that called us out of nothingness was our first step towards the fulfilment of our calling, that God should be in all and that we should be in him as he is in us.

We must be prepared to find that the last step of our

relationship with God is an act of pure adoration, face to face with a mystery into which we cannot enter. We grow into the knowledge of God gradually from year to year until the end of our life and we will continue to do so through all eternity, without coming to a point when we shall be able to say that now we know all that is knowable of God. This process of the gradual discovery of God leads us at every moment to stand with our past experience behind us and the mystery of God knowable and still unknown before us. The little we know of God makes it difficult for us to learn more, because the more cannot simply be added to the little, since every meeting brings such a change of perspective that what was known before becomes almost untrue in the light of what is known later.

This is true of any knowledge which we acquire; every day teaches us something in science or the humanities, but the learning we have acquired makes sense only because it brings us to the borderline beyond which there is something we can still discover. If we stop just to rehearse what we know, we shall waste our time. So the first thing, if we want to meet the real God in prayer, is to realise that all the knowledge previously acquired has brought us to stand before him. All this is precious and meaningful, but if we go no farther it becomes ghostly, phantom-like, it will cease to be real life; it will be a memory and one cannot live on memories.

In our relations with people we turn inevitably just one facet of our personality to one facet of the other person's; it may be good when it is a way of establishing contact, it may be evil when we do so to exploit the other person's weaknesses. To God also we turn the facet which is closest

to him, the trusting or loving side. But we must be aware
of the fact that it is never a facet of God we meet: we meet
God in his entirety.

When we come to pray we hope to experience God as
someone who is present and that our prayer will be, if not
a dialogue, at least a discourse to someone who listens. We
are afraid that we may sense no presence at all and have the
impression of speaking in the void, with no one there to
listen, to answer, to be interested. But this would be a
purely subjective impression; if we compare our experience
of prayer with our normal daily human contacts, we know
that someone may be listening very intently to what we
say and yet we may feel that our words are being poured
out in vain. Our prayer always reaches God but it is not
always answered by a sense of joy or peace.

When we speak in terms of taking a stand, we always
think that here we are and there is God, outside us. If we
search for God, above, or in front, or around us, we will
not find him. St John Chrysostom said: 'Find the door of
the inner chamber of your soul and you will discover that
this is the door into the kingdom of Heaven.' St Ephraim
of Syria says that God, when he created man, put in the
deepest part of him all the kingdom, and that the problem
of human life is to dig deep enough to come upon the
hidden treasure. Therefore, to find God we must dig in
search of this inner chamber, of this place where the whole
kingdom of God is present at the very core of us, where
God and we can meet. The best tool, the one which will
go through all obstacles, is prayer. The problem is one of
praying attentively, simply and truthfully without replacing the real God by any false God, by an idol, by a product

of our imagination and without trying to have a preview of any mystical experience. Concentrating on what we say, believing that every word we pronounce reaches God, we can use our own words or the words of greater men to express, better than we could, what we feel or what we sense dimly within us. It is not in a multitude of words that we shall be heard by God but in their veracity. When we use our own words we must speak to God with precision, neither trying to be short nor trying to be long, but trying to be true.

There are moments when prayers are spontaneous and easy, others when it feels as if the spring has dried up. This is the time to use the prayers of other men which express basically what we believe, all those things which are not at present made vivid by any deep response of the heart. Then we must pray in a double act of faith, not only faith in God but also in ourselves, trusting in the faith which is dimmed, in spite of its being part of us.

There are times when we do not need any words of prayer, neither our own nor anyone else's and then we pray in perfect silence. This perfect silence is the ideal prayer, provided, however, that the silence is real and not daydreaming. We have very little experience of what deep silence of body and soul means, when complete serenity fills the soul, when complete peace fills the body, when there is no turmoil or stirring of any sort and when we stand before God, completely open in an act of adoration. There may be times when we feel physically well and mentally relaxed, tired of words because we have used so many of them already; we do not want to stir and we feel happy in this fragile balance; this is on the borderline of slipping into daydreaming. Inner silence is absence of any sort of inward stirring of thought or emotion, but it is complete alertness, openness to God. We must keep complete silence when we can, but never allow it to degenerate into simple contentment. To prevent this the great writers of Orthodoxy warn us never to abandon completely the normal forms of prayer, because even those who reached this contemplative silence found it necessary, whenever they were in danger of spiritual slackness, to reintroduce words of prayer until prayer had renewed silence.

The Greek Fathers set this silence, which they called *hesychia*, both as the starting-point and the final achievement of a life of prayer. Silence is the state in which all the powers of the soul and all the faculties of the body are completely at peace, quiet and recollected, perfectly alert yet free from any turmoil or agitation. A simile which we find in many writings of the Fathers is that of the waters of a pond. As long as there are ripples on the surface, nothing can be reflected properly, neither the trees nor the sky; when the surface is quite still, the sky is perfectly reflected, the trees on the bank and everything is there as distinct as in reality.

Another simile of the same sort used by the Fathers is that as long as the mud which is at the bottom of a pond has not settled, the water is not clear and one can see nothing through it. These two analogies apply to the state of the human heart. 'Blessed are the pure in heart for they shall see God' (Mt 5:8). As long as the mud is in motion in the water there is no clear vision through it, and again as long as the surface is covered with ripples there can be no adequate reflection of what surrounds the pond.

As long as the soul is not still there can be no vision, but when stillness has brought us into the presence of God, then another sort of silence, much more absolute, intervenes: the silence of a soul that is not only still and recollected but which is overawed in an act of worship by God's presence; a silence in which, as Julian of Norwich puts it, 'Prayer oneth the soul to God.'

EPILOGUE*

Prayer for Beginners

WE ARE ALL beginners and I do not intend to give you a course of lectures, but I wish to share with you some of the things I have learned, partly by experience, and probably more through the experiences of others.

Prayer is essentially an encounter, a meeting between a soul and God, but to be real an encounter takes two persons each being really himself. To a very great extent we are unreal and God so often in our relationship is unreal to us because we believe that we turn to God, when we are in fact turning to something we imagine to be God; and we think that we are standing before him in all truth, whereas we are putting forward someone who is not our real self, who is an actor, a sham, a stage personality. Every one of us is a variety of persons at the same time; it may be a very rich blending, but also it may be an unfortunate meeting of discordant personalities. We are different according to circumstances and surroundings: the various people that meet us know us as different persons.

* From the BBC television series 'The Epilogue', first shown in 1958.

H

There is a Russian proverb that says, 'He is a lion when meeting sheep, but he is a sheep when he meets lions.' Which is quite true in more ways than one: we all know the lady who is all smiles with outsiders and who is a holy terror at home, or the big boss who is so tame in private life.

When it comes to praying, our first difficulty is to find which one of our personalities should be put forward to meet God. It is not simple because we are so unaccustomed to be our real self that in all truth we do not know which one that is; and we do not know how to find it. But if we were to give a few minutes a day to think over our various activities and contacts, we would probably come much closer to the discovery. We could find out the sort of person we were when we met so and so, and the other person we were when we were doing this or that. And we could ask ourselves: but when was I really myself? Perhaps never, perhaps only for a split second or perhaps to a certain extent under special circumstances, while meeting particular people. Now, in these five or ten minutes which you can spare, and I am sure everyone can spare them in the course of the day, you will discover that there is nothing more boring for us than to be left alone with ourselves! We usually live some sort of reflected life. Not only are we a variety of people successively under various circumstances but also the very life that is in us belongs so often to other people. If you look into yourself, and if you dare to question how often you act from the very core of your personality, how often you are expressing your own self, you will see that it happens rarely enough. Too often we are immersed in what is happening around us, all the unnecessaries we gather from the wireless, television, newspapers, but during this period, these few minutes of concentration, we must shed everything that is not essential to life.

Then of course you run the risk of remaining bored with yourself; all right, be bored. But this does not mean that there is nothing left in us, because at rock bottom we are made in the image of God, and this stripping is very much like the cleaning of an ancient, beautiful wall painting, or of a painting by a great master that was painted over in the course of the centuries by tasteless people who had intruded upon the real beauty that had been created by the master. To begin with, the more we clean, the more things disappear, and it seems to us that we have created a mess where there was at least a certain amount of beauty; perhaps not much, but some beauty. And then we begin to discover the real beauty which the great master has put into his painting; we see the misery, then the mess in between, but at the same time we have a preview of the authentic beauty. And we discover that what we are is a poor person who needs God; but not God to fill the gap – God to be met.

So let us set out to do this and let us also every evening of this week, pray a very simple prayer:

'Help me, O God, to put off all pretences and to find my true self.'

Grief and joy, both great gifts of God, are often the meeting point with our real self, when monkey tricks are put aside and when we become invulnerable, out of reach of the falsities of life.

Next we have to investigate the problem of the real God,

because obviously if we are to address God, this God must be real. We all know what a headmaster is for schoolboys; when they have to go and see him they go to the head-master and it never occurs to them until they have grown up and no longer in his power that the headmaster is a man. They think of him in terms of a function; but this empties his human personality of every human characteristic and there can be no kind of human contact with him.

Another example: when a boy is in love with a girl, he adorns her with all sorts of perfections; but she may not have any of them and this person constructed out of nothing is very often 'nothing', clad in qualities that are artificial. Here again there can be no contact because the boy is addressing someone who does not exist. This is true also of God. We have a lot of mental or visual pictures of God, collected from books, from church, from what we hear from adults when we are children and eventually from clergymen when we are older. Quite often these pictures prevent us from meeting the real God. They are not quite false because there is some truth in them, and yet they are perfectly inadequate to the reality of God. If we wish to meet God we must, on the one hand, make use of the knowledge acquired either personally, or by means of reading, hearing, listening, but also, go farther.

The knowledge of God which we possess today is a result of yesterday's experience and if we set ourselves in front of God as we know him, we will always turn our backs to the present and to the future, looking only at our own past. It is not God that we are going to meet, it is what we have already learned about him. This illustrates the function of theology, since theology is our whole knowledge of God and not the small amount we have personally already known and learned about him. You must, if you wish to meet God as he really is, come to him with a certain experience, allow it to bring you close to God, and leave it at that, standing before not the God you know but the God both known and unknown.

What will happen next? Something quite simple: God who is free to come to you, to respond, to answer your prayers, may come to you and make you feel, perceive, his presence; he may also choose not to do so. He may just give you a sense of his real absence, and this experience is as important as the other, because in both cases you come upon the reality of God's right to answer or to stand back.

Try, then, to discover your own real self and to stand it face to face with God as he is, having shed all false images or idols of God; and to help you in this search, to give you support in this effort, I suggest that you should, this week, pray the following prayer:

'Help me, O God, to discard all false pictures of thee, whatever the cost to my comfort.'

In the search for our true self we may come not only to boredom, which I have mentioned, but to fear, or even to despair. It is this nakedness that brings us to our senses; then we can begin to pray. The first thing to avoid is lying to God; it seems quite obvious, and yet we do not always observe it. Let us speak frankly to God, say to him what sort of person we are; not that he does not know it, but there is a great difference between assuming that someone we love knows all about us, and having the courage and real love for the person to speak truthfully and tell every-thing about ourselves. Let us say to God openly that we stand before him with a feeling of uneasiness, that we do not really want to meet him, that we are tired and would rather go to bed, but we must beware of being frivolous or just presumptuous: he remains our God. After that the ideal would be to remain happily in his presence, as when we are with people we love dearly, when there is real intimacy. But more often than not we are not on those terms with God. We do not feel so happy and intimate with him as to be able just to sit and look at him and feel glad. As we must talk, let it be genuine talk. Let us put all our worries to God, squarely, and then, having told him every-thing, so that he should know them from us, we should drop them, leave them to him. Now that he is in the know, it is no longer any of our concern: we can freely think of him.

The exercise of this week, obviously, must be added to the exercises of the previous weeks, and it will consist in learning to put everyone of our concerns to God, after having settled ourselves in front of him, and then drop these concerns; and to help us in this, let us from day to day repeat a very simple and precise prayer, that will define our way of dealing with God:

'Help me O God to let go all my problems, and fix my mind on thee.'

If we did not put our worries to God, they would stand between him and us in the course of our meeting, but we have also just seen that the next move, which is essential, is to drop them. We should make that in an act of confidence, trusting God enough to give him the troubles we wish to get off our shoulders. But then, what next? We seem to have emptied ourselves, there is nothing much left, what are we going to do? We cannot remain empty, because if we do we shall be filled by the wrong things, by feelings, thoughts, emotions and reminiscences and so on. We must, I believe, remember that an encounter is not meant to be a one-sided discourse on our part. Conversation means not only talking but hearing what the other has to say. And to achieve this we must learn to be silent; although it seems trifling it is a very important point.

I remember that one of the first people who came to me for advice when I was ordained was an old lady who said: 'Father, I have been praying almost unceasingly for fourteen years, and I have never had any sense of God's presence.' So I said: 'Did you give him a chance to put in a word?' 'Oh well,' she said. 'No, I have been talking to him all the time, because is not that prayer?' I said: 'No, I do not think it is, and what I suggest is that you should set apart fifteen minutes a day, sit and just knit before the face of God.' And so she did. What was the result? Quite soon she came again and said: 'It is extraordinary, when I pray to God, in other words when I talk to him, I feel nothing, but when I sit quietly, face to face with him, then I feel wrapped in his presence.' You will never be able to pray to God really and from all your heart unless you learn to keep silent and rejoice in the miracle of his presence, or if you prefer, of your being face to face with him although you do not see him.

Quite often, having said what we have to say and having sat for a certain time, we are at a loss: what shall we do?

What we should do I believe is to start on some set prayers. Some find set prayers too easy, and at the same time see a danger of taking for actual praying the repetition of what someone else has said in the past. Indeed, if it is just mechanical it is not worth doing, but what is overlooked is that it depends on us whether it is mechanical or not, by paying attention to the words we say. Others complain that set prayers would be unreal because it is not quite what they would express, it is not theirs. In a sense it is unreal, but only in the same way in which the painting of a great master is unreal for a schoolboy, or the music of a great composer is unreal for a beginner, and yet that is just the point: we go to concerts, we visit art galleries to learn what real music or real painting is, to form our taste; and that is partly why we should use set prayers, to learn which feelings, which thoughts, which ways of expressions we should employ, if we belong to the Church. It also helps in time of dryness, when we have very little to say.

Apart from the stripped, naked, reduced-to-bone person which we are when we remain just alone, we are also in the image of God and the child of God that is in each of us is capable of praying with the loftiest and holiest prayers of the Church. We must remember that and make use of them. I suggest we add to the exercises we have been doing, a period of silence, a few minutes – three or four minutes – which we shall end with a prayer:

'Help me, O God, to see my own sins, never to judge my neighbour, and may the glory all be thine!'

Before I enter into the subject of 'Unanswered Prayer', I would like to pray to God that he might enlighten both me and you, because it is a difficult subject, yet such a vital one. It is one of the great temptations which everyone may meet on his way, which makes it very hard for beginners, and even for proficient people, to pray to God. Many times people pray and it seems to them that they are addressing an empty heaven; quite often it is because their prayer is meaningless, childish.

I remember the case of an old man telling me that when he was a child he prayed for several months that he would be given by God the amazing gift which his uncle possessed – that of every evening taking his teeth out of his mouth, and putting them into a glass of water – and he was terribly happy later on that God did not grant his wish. Often our prayers are as puerile as this, and of course they are not granted. Quite frequently when we pray we believe that we are praying rightly, but we pray for something which involves other people, of whom we do not think at all. If we pray for wind in our sails, we do not realise that it may mean a storm at sea for others, and God will not grant a request that affects others badly.

Besides these two obvious points, there is another side to unanswered prayer which is more basic and deep: there are cases when we pray to God from all our heart for something which, from every angle, seems to be worthy of being heard, and yet there is nothing but silence, and silence is much harder to bear than refusal. If God said 'No', it would be a positive reaction of God's, but silence is, as it were, the absence of God and that leads us to two temptations: when our prayer is not answered, we either doubt God, or else we doubt ourselves. What we doubt in God is not his might, his power to do what we wish, but we doubt his love, his concern. We beg for something essential and he does not even seem to be concerned; where is his love and his compassion? This is the first temptation.

There is another: we know that if we had as much faith as a mustard seed, we could move mountains and when we see that nothing budges, we think, 'Does that mean that the faith I have got is adulterated, false?' This again is untrue, and there is another answer: if you read the gospel attentively, you will see that there is only one prayer in it that was not answered. It is the prayer of Christ in the garden of Gethsemane, and yet we know that if once in history God was concerned for the one who prayed, it was then for his son, before his death, and also we know that if ever perfect faith was exemplified, it was in his case, but God found that the faith of the divine sufferer was great enough to bear silence.

God withholds an answer to our prayers not only when they are unworthy but when he finds in us such greatness, such depth – depth and power of faith – that he can rely upon us to remain faithful even in the face of his silence.

I remember a young woman with an incurable disease and after years of the awareness of God's presence, she suddenly sensed God's absence – some sort of real absence – and she wrote to me saying, 'Pray to God, please, that I should never yield to the temptation of building up an illusion of his presence, rather than accept his absence.' Her faith was great. She was able to stand this temptation and God gave her this experience of his silent absence.

Remember these examples, think them over because one day you will surely have to face the same situation.

I cannot give you any exercise, but I only want you to

remember that we should always keep our faith intact, both in the love of God and in our honest, truthful faith, and when this temptation comes upon us, let us say this prayer, which is made of two sentences pronounced by Jesus Christ himself:

'Into Thy hands I commend my spirit,
Thy Will, not mine, be done.'

Whatever I have tried to give as an outline of the main ways in which we should approach prayer, does it mean that if you do all I have suggested you will be able to pray? Indeed not, because prayer is not simply an effort which we can make the moment we intend to pray; prayer must be rooted in our life and if our life contradicts our prayers, or if our prayers have nothing to do with our life, they will never be alive nor real. Of course we can deal with that difficulty and make an easy escape by excluding from our prayers everything that, in our life, does not fit into the framework of prayer – all those things we are ashamed or uneasy about. But it does not solve anything satisfactorily.

Another difficulty which we meet constantly is to fall into daydreaming, when our prayer expresses a sentimental trend and is not the expression of what our life is basically. There is one common solution for these two difficulties; that of joining together life and prayer, making them one, by living our prayer. To help us along this line, set prayers, of which I have already spoken, are most precious because they are an objective, hard outline of a way of praying. You may say that they are unnatural, and it is true in the sense that they express the life of people who are im-measurably greater than we are, of real christians, but that is just why you can make use of them, trying to become the sort of people for whom those prayers are natural.

You remember Christ's words: 'Into Thy hands I commend my Spirit.' Of course it is not within our own experience, but if we learn from day to day to become the sort of person who is capable of pronouncing these words sincerely, in all honesty, we will not only make our prayers real, but we will make ourselves real, with a new reality, the true reality of becoming the sons of God.

If you take, for instance, the five prayers which I have suggested and if you take one after the other, each of the petitions of these prayers, and if you try to make each of them in turn the motto, the slogan that will direct the day, you will see that prayer becomes the criterion of your life; it will give you a framework for it, but also your life will stand in judgement, against you or for you, giving you the lie when you pronounce these words, or, on the contrary, affirming that you are true to them. Take each sentence of each prayer and make it the rule of one day after the other, so for weeks and weeks, until you become the sort of person for whom these words are life.

We have to part now; I have immensely enjoyed being with you, although I do not see you, but we are united in prayer and in our common interest for the life of the spirit. May the Lord God be with each of you and in our midst for ever.

And before we part, I would like us to say together one short prayer that will unite us before the throne of God:

O Lord, I know not what to ask of thee; thou alone knowest what are my true needs. Thou lovest me more than I know how to love myself. Help me to see my real needs which are concealed from me. I dare not ask either a cross or consolation. I can only wait on thee. My heart is open to thee. Visit and help me for thy great mercy's sake, strike me and heal me, cast me down and raise me up. I worship in silence thy holy will and thine inscrutable ways. I offer myself as a sacrifice to thee. I put all my trust in thee. I have no other desire than to fulfil thy will. Teach me how to pray, pray thou thyself in me.

AMEN